The
Job Seekers Guide
for
Extraverts & Introverts

Advice for Boomers, Gen Xers and Millennials

By
Carol A. Linden
MBTI (Myers-Briggs) Master Practitioner

FONTLIFE PUBLICATIONS

The Job Seekers Guide for Extraverts & Introverts
Advice for Boomers, Gen Xers and Millennials
by Carol A. Linden

A FontLife Publication, LLC
Raleigh, NC 27603
http://fontlifepublications.com/

Copyright © 2014 Carol A. Linden

All rights reserved solely by the copyright holder. The copyright holder guarantees all contents are original and do not infringe upon the legal rights of any other person or work. No part of this book may be reproduced or transmitted in any form or by any means, electronic or mechanical, including photocopying, recording or by any information storage and retrieval system, without the permission of the copyright holder. The views expressed in this book are not necessarily those of the publisher.

Edition ISBNs:
Softcover: ISBN-10: 1-62422025-8
              ISBN-13: 978-1-62422-025-8
Kindle: ISBN-10: 1-62422026-6
              ISBN-13: 978-1-62422-026-5

First Edition 2014
Printed in the United States of America

Library of Congress Control Number: 2014950315

Original Cover Art by Mike R. Neel

Author Photo by Charles Gupton of Charles Gupton Photography and by Lynae Thomas of Style by Lynae.

Dedication

This small volume is dedicated to all the job seekers who've inspired me and uplifted me as they've come through the Colonial Job Seekers weekly networking meetings. These are people who have faced their challenge with some trepidation but also with faith and hope and who have reached out to encourage and help others during a very challenging time.

To those who are purchasing this book, may this small volume, based on both my own job transition as well as 4 years of volunteer work, be pragmatic and helpful to you, save you valuable time, and make your job search more effective and your job transition briefer.

May your job search be a sprint instead of a marathon. But if it is a marathon, may this small volume help lift you up and give you information that helps you endure it with as much dignity and grace as possible while helping others along the way.

To paraphrase what I say to my group at Colonial Job Seekers networking program every Monday morning, "I'm whole-heartedly sorry that you need this book, but since you do need it, I'm glad if through it I can be of service to you."

All of us who have experienced job transitions during "the great recession" will be better and stronger people because of it. I am convinced of that, and I will go to my grave grateful for the abilities it has developed in me that I had no idea I was capable of. I'm also grateful for all of the amazing professionals I have met along the way that I would never have otherwise known.

This experience will not kill us; it will just feel like it's going to at times.

Table of Contents

Introduction—How to Use This Book:
    A Guide for the Generations vi
Chapter 1—Job Seeker Basics:
    Nine Things You Really Have to Do 9
Chapter 2—Are You Introverted or Extraverted and
    Why It Matters.. 20
Chapter 3—Taking Care of Yourself during the Job Search 25
Chapter 4—Networking: It's for All of Us Now 35
Chapter 5—Networking Tips for Introverts 39
Chapter 6—Networking Tips for Extraverts... 45
Chapter 7—Resumes.. 51
Chapter 8—Interview Tips for Introverts 57
Chapter 9—Interview Tips for Extraverts... 64
Chapter 10—Your 30-Second Elevator Speech 71
Chapter 11—When You Don't Know What You Want to Do Next 75
Chapter 12—Working with Recruiters... 81
Chapter 13—Hindsight is 20/20 85
Chapter 14—Especially for Millennials:
    How to Get into the Job Market 91
Recommended Resources 97
About the Author 107

Acknowledgments

Without Paula Bryan and my colleagues on the Colonial Job Seekers Network leadership team at Colonial Baptist Church in Cary, NC, I would never have gotten the chance to be part of this uplifting volunteer work. It continues to both inspire and develop me. I am very grateful to my Baptist colleagues for allowing my Episcopal self to serve side-by-side with them.

Without my publisher and colleague Victor Font, this book would not now be in your hands (virtually or physically). Thank you, Victor, for your skill and for your generosity in taking on a new author.

Without my editor Jonah Womack, this book would be less skillfully written and would, shall we say, meander a bit. I don't care if you're F. Scott Fitzgerald himself, every writer needs a good editor. Jonah is my very own Maxwell Perkins and I am grateful for him every day.

I might not have made it through the job transition as sanely as I did without my dearest friends and supporters, Coye (both mother and friend), Jan and Mitch, Larry and Charlotte, Deborah and Gary, Dave, Kavita, Mary Ann and Nancy, Donna, Patty and Peggy. Thanks to Lilly, Mary, Ed, Sue, Craig and Jake for helping me transition into a successful independent. Thank you all from the bottom of my heart for hanging in there with me and seeing me through this "may you live in interesting times" experience.

Introduction—How to Use This Book: A Guide for the Generations

This book contains valuable material for Baby Boomers, Gen Xers, and Millennials alike, because they are all experiencing unemployment during this recession. The economy is struggling to recover so that life can get back to normal, whatever normal is going to look like in the 21st century.

With that said, here are some pointers so you don't miss something written especially for your generation.

Baby Boomers

Most of this book is for you. You probably know the reasons new techniques are necessary, but if you're newly in the job market, you may not. I'll list a few key reasons here:

- Age discrimination is real. You need ways around it and techniques in this book will help you do just that.
- The job transition period is longer for Boomers than for other age groups. I'm not saying that's fair. It just is what it is. The chapters on taking care of yourself can help you get through this time more gracefully and with more sanity.
- If you were at one company for a long time, you may not be aware of how much has changed. You need to know about *functional resumes* and *behavioral interviews*.
- Boomers are not so much being rejected as *not being seen* due to the onslaught of applications and resumes. You need to know how to use *networking* to *get eyes on* your resume and application.

The chapter especially labeled for Millennials is not for you. If you have children who are out of work, however, you might want to read that chapter. They are experiencing unemployment at levels over 30%. Their struggles are different from yours, but they are struggling, too.

If you want another job in a field you have immediate and relevant experience in, you may find **Chapter 12—Working with Recruiters** useful. If, however, you're tired of what you were doing and want to reinvent yourself, a recruiter is not the route for you. Instead see **Chapter 11—When You Don't Know What You Want to Do Next.**

Gen Xers

Like Boomers, this book is also for you. Though your time between layoff and landing will probably be shorter than it is for Boomers—I get no pleasure in saying that, but it's in the data—it will still probably be longer than you want it to be. You think, "I'm young, I'm talented, I'm good at what I do, this is a piece of cake. I'll be back at work within two to three months." I wish for you with all my heart that that's true. In this economy, even you are likely facing a longer search period than you hoped for.

While you do not face age discrimination, there are still three people looking for every one job opening, and the length of your job search will be impacted. Also, with so many applicants, you, too, will need to use 21st century required techniques such as "getting eyes on" your resume and networking your way inside organizations.

Chapter 14—Especially for Millennials: How to Get into the Job Market does not apply to you. *Chapter 3—Taking Care of Yourself during the Job Search* may not apply to you as much as it does to Boomers. Still, if the job transition period is long for you, that can hit your self-esteem and even you may find useful ideas in *Chapter 3—Taking Care of Yourself during the Job Search.* Take heart! You will land, just probably not as quickly as you'd like. Age is not a barrier for you. That said, you will still have to apply yourself and do due diligence to hasten your landing.

Remember, this is a new world. You will not only have more downtime between jobs, but also change jobs more often than you'd like. It's okay. It's not about you. It's about a changing world. My best advice for you is to

1. Use this book to help hasten your landing!
2. Build your network and keep it going even when you're employed. The strength of your network is your best ally in this

brave new world of more frequent job transitions.
3. Keep your skills updated, even if you have to pay for it yourself. It's no longer viable to expect an employer to keep you relevant and look after your career. Those days are past. Plan your own career and stay relevant.

Millennials

Most of this book will also be very useful to you. In fact, the only material that may not apply to you is **Chapter 3—Taking Care of Yourself during the Job Search.** Even though you're probably not dealing with layoffs, getting into the market at all in this economy is a struggle, and you may face similar frustrations and hits to your self-esteem that would make even that chapter useful to you. You're making a transition, too. Transitioning from school to the professional world can be as much of a shock to your system as transitioning from working to layoffs is to Boomers.

I've also written a special chapter just for you: **Chapter 14—Especially for Millennials: How to Get into the Job Market**. The chapters on using recruiters may not apply to you because you may not have enough job experience yet for recruiters to be much of an option. That said, if you're in your late 20s or early 30s, you may have enough serious experience in one field to consider a recruiter. If that is the case, see **Chapter 12—Working with Recruiters.**

Chapter 1 — Job Seeker Basics: Nine Things You Really Have to Do

Here are some very basic things to remember as you begin your job transition.

1. Don't go through it alone—get support
2. Face the "shame gremlin" head-on
3. Retool yourself for a 21st century job search
4. Manage your challenging feelings without getting stuck in them
5. Show up as your best self in an interview
6. Be an encouraging and positive force when you network
7. Get an accountability partner—*not* your significant other
8. Take good physical care of yourself so that you can keep getting out there
9. Keep your spirits up, mind your attitude

1. Don't go through it alone—get support

Job Seeker Groups: Many others are in the same boat that you are. See that you are not alone. Join job seeker networking groups.

These groups can be found all over the country. There are many types. Try a few. Don't give up until you find the right one for you. Some focus more on building relationships through networking. Other groups primarily hold skill-based workshops on topics like building your resume, performing well in interviews, and communicating with recruiters. Go to these. They often have very knowledgeable speakers and can help make your efforts more pointed and productive. Don't shun groups that are mostly made up of the unemployed. People who are unemployed can still have very valuable connections into companies you're targeting.

I facilitate for a job seekers group that I found through the grapevine. The two largest groups in my area just kept coming up over and over again when I talked to people. Once I found those, they had lists of other groups in the area. You can also check with whatever your state calls their employment security commission. From my experimenting, I've found that searching the Internet for phrases like these can yield good results and help you find groups in your area:

> job seeker groups <*your-town*>
> job seeker networking groups
> job seeker support groups

Often the larger churches in your area may conduct job seekers outreach programs. Some groups focus especially on helping you find opportunities for networking. You never know where your next connection will come from, or where the next introduction will lead. See ***Chapter 5—Networking Tips for Introverts*** or ***Chapter 6—Networking Tips for Extraverts.***

Community Colleges: Also look to your local community college. In my area a department there runs state-reimbursed programs that allow them to offer certain kinds of classes at no cost to anyone who has been laid off, has been given notice of being laid off, or is currently under-employed. They typically offer classes on topics such as "reinventing yourself," social media, LinkedIn, resumes, personal branding, and interviewing skills. These programs can be invaluable. They can help you make progress much more quickly and with fewer faltering steps as you seek full employment again.

Professional Groups: By all means, continue going to meetings and workshops run by professional groups in your field. If you don't already belong to one or more of these, check them out in your area. They typically hold meetings and workshops on topics that will help you stay up to date in your profession. Examples include organizations for professional project managers, engineers, IT professionals, finance professionals, technical writers, and trainers. Attend these programs and workshops. Stay in touch with those in your profession, as it will show a potential employer that you're staying relevant in your field. As a side benefit, you may also find out about job openings that you haven't noticed yet or that haven't even been listed yet.

2. Face the "shame gremlin" head-on

Tell people you are looking for work. Out of misguided shame, job seekers often neglect to tell others in their neighborhoods, churches, clubs, professional groups, and work circles. that they are out of work. But here's the problem: how will anyone know to inform you of an opening or to keep an eye out if you don't admit that you're looking for a job?

This is a moment in history. As of early 2015, millions of baby boomers are still out of work. One third of Millennials are unemployed, and even those who are employed are likely still living in their parents' house because it's hard to find jobs that pay them enough to be able to move out. There is *nothing* to be ashamed of. Countless hard-working, worthy, capable people are out of work right now. Remember that. There are tough days that you will need to remind yourself of this in the face of the return of the "shame gremlins."

There are, at the time of this writing, three job seekers for every one job opening. The market is competitive and you are up against difficult odds—not impossible odds, but challenging odds. There is no shame in this. You're going to have to let go of shame to move forward and reach out to others.

When feeling discouraged, call a friend you trust–but choose that friend carefully. As researcher and author Brené Brown says, choose someone who has "earned the right to hear your story." In my own experience, this someone will have the skill to listen compassionately without trying to "fix" or judge the situation. There are many people who love you. But, try as they might, a lot of them do not have the skill to "hear your story," to handle a phone call in which you vent about how bad you feel and how hard things are for you right now. Forgive the ones who don't have this skill; call the ones who do.

3. Retool yourself for a 21st century job search

If you're a Boomer, yes, things have probably changed a lot since you were last on the job market. Take a deep breath. You can do this. The process will probably take longer than in the past and the interview will be less of a historical interview and more of a behavioral one. (See "Interview" below.)

If you're a Millennial, today's world is not the same as when your parents entered the workforce. If it seems to them that you're "not trying hard enough," please be patient with them. The job scene most likely looked very different when they were first searching for work. (Unless they were searching for work during one of the several mini-recessions that preceded the near catastrophic one of 2008.)

Here are four ways to retool yourself for a 21st century job search:

1. **Update your resume:**

- If you were laid off and your company offers outplacement services, *do* take them up on it. Getting your resume in shape is one thing they'll help you with.
- Look for free classes at your local community college and local state employment offices. Look on the Internet. Go to the library.
- **Boomers:** You probably need to do more than just brush off the old one and add the latest job. You need a *functional resume* in addition to the traditional historical resume. Look this term up online. Buy a book or get the help of a professional. Most people will need this new kind of resume moving forward.
- **Millennials:** You need a functional resume too, but for a different reason. You're not trying to hide an age-revealing job history. You're trying to compile all your experience and demonstrate how it makes you perfect for a job you've never held. It can be done.
- **If you are a Millennial, consider unpaid internships.** Your challenge may be to have relevant experience for the job that you really want. Internships are wonderful for that. Even if you have to take an unpaid one and work a "survival job" to get by, it will be worth it. Actual experience is worth its weight in gold. Seek out an organization, profit or not-for-profit that you are interested in and talk to someone about interning. Both of you will benefit. (BTW, delivering mail is not a legitimate unpaid internship; skill-building work that helps build your professional resume *is* a legitimate unpaid internship.)

2. **Get out there and network**

- Get out there and become part of a larger community. You will be amazed at all the generous and talented people you are going to meet. We will all be more connected after this experience, painful and scary as the experience can be at times.
- If you are a Boomer, yes, the last time you were "out there," networking probably wasn't necessary. It's required now. Unless you want to send your applications into the deep, dark vortex of the Internet, never hearing anything back, then you've got to put yourself out there, get connected, and seek help "getting eyes on" your resume.
- It's not that you're being rejected. It's that you're *not being seen*. There are still three unemployed for every one job opening. HR professionals are still overwhelmed with the onslaught. You need human eyes on your resume. Networking can get you that.
- Be willing to offer this same kindness/service to others. Be willing to contact someone you know inside an organization, introduce someone, help them get an interest interview, or help pass their resume to someone who can do them some good by seeing it. It's called "paying it forward." Go out there with the attitude, "How can I help you?" More on this later.

3. **Prepare for Behavioral Interviews**

- The interview will *not* be a historical set of "what did you do" questions; it will start right off the bat with *behavioral questions*. Something like, "Tell me about a time when you had a problem with a co-worker (or your manager) and how you resolved it." This is a new ballgame. Prepare, prepare, prepare for these questions.
- Google "64 Hardest Interview Questions." It's all over the Internet. Pick an article that includes suggestions for how to answer. Taking on 64 questions at once can seem overwhelming, so practice five a day until you've covered them all.
- Do not underestimate the importance of the phone interview. It's not just *pro forma* any more. It's a serious screening tool. They will start with the behavioral questions as a screening tool.
- See one of these two chapters: ***Chapter 8—Interview Tips for Introverts*** or ***Chapter 9—Interview Tips for Extraverts***.

4. **Yes, you do need to be on www.LinkedIn.com**

- With the exception of some conservative banking institutions, 21st century professionals need to have a presence on LinkedIn, with up-to-date information and a professional-looking photo. (That means no baseball caps, no Golden Retrievers, no ski boats. Unless, of course, those are integral to your work.)
- Look to your local community colleges or job centers for classes in LinkedIn. It's not hard at all; with a little bit of help, you can be in and up and running in no time.
- When you get steady on your feet in LinkedIn, you'll even learn how to use the platform to search for jobs and get eyes on your resume inside a company you've targeted.

4. Manage your challenging feelings

Some pretty strong feelings can run through you, especially if your job transition period is more like a marathon than a sprint. This can be especially true if the period right before you left your last job was stressful or even painful. We can leave situations like this with open wounds. Those have to be tended and healed before we're ready to interview for new jobs.

Classic pitfalls to watch for when dealing with challenging feelings like grief, anger, pity, and resentment:

- Classic Pitfall 1: getting mired down in negative feelings
- Classic Pitfall 2: stuffing away your negative feelings

You cannot afford to get stuck in either of these pits. But let's be realists. You are going to fall into them—both of them. You just need to know how to climb out of these pits after each time you fall into them.

As tempting as it may be and as warranted as it may feel, you simply cannot afford to get mired down in a pity party or stuck in your anger or bitterness. It's just not going to help you move forward and get hired again.

You also cannot afford to ignore your feelings and pretend they're not there. They tend to come out in ways and at times that backfire or they just drain us.

How to deal with these pitfalls? They both have the same answer, really:

> *Feel* the feelings, then let them go.
> Don't get stuck in them.
> Don't stuff them.

One of the reasons we tend to avoid negative feelings is that we're afraid if we let ourselves feel them, we'll get stuck and won't be able to get out of them. Actually, the opposite is true. It takes energy to hold the feelings inside, and that just drains us of energy we need for the job search. Remember as a kid being in a swimming pool or the ocean and trying to hold a beach ball under the water? Remember how difficult it was to keep it submerged? You'd always lose control at some point and the ball would shoot out from under you? Your submerged feelings are like that. And they tend to pick inconvenient times to shoot out of your control,

We also try to stuff negative feelings because we're just plain afraid of the pain. Seriously, who would *want* to feel those awful feelings? Just know that we are all afraid of that pain; you're not alone. Feeling the fear and anger and resentment won't kill you—it only feels like it will, at times.

Another reason *not* to just stuff feelings is that they will run us ragged, so we actually get stuck by trying to run from them without feeling them. In the same way that exercise burns off fat and cleanses your body of debris, consciously acknowledging negative feelings helps to burn them off, releasing that emotional energy and actually freeing us to get on with our day and concentrate better.

The trick is to let ourselves feel the hurt, the fear, the anger. Then let them go. They will come and go in waves as we heal, and that's normal. (I'm not saying it feels good; I'm just saying it's normal.) Just don't allow yourself to get trapped in a vicious cycle of anger and resentment. That's not burning them off. Feel the pain, let it burn itself off and subside. Then you can get on with your day.

Christopher Reeve, who, after a tragic horse-riding accident, spent the last nine years of his life as a quadriplegic, said in an interview something that I will never forget. Every morning he spent 10 minutes feeling sorry for himself. Then that was it for the day—no more pity party. He just got on with his life. If Christopher Reeve could pull that off, surely I can ask the same of myself. All I lost was a job.

5. Show up as your best self in an interview

One of the ways you do this is to practice, practice, practice. Yes, adults may be tired of hearing that, but practice really does increase skill level. Interviews can be few and far between during difficult times. You deserve the chance to show up as your best self, so practice ahead of time so that you'll be prepared.

- Practice your answers to the "64 Toughest Interview Questions." You won't be taken off-guard if you've done your homework ahead of time and are ready to take on difficult behavioral questions.
- Practice out loud and in front of a mirror. Yes, it will feel silly and awkward. But it really works. Just saying it inside your head is not good enough preparation. You can also ask fellow job seekers and colleagues to help you practice.
- **Smile**. The interviewer can hear the smile in your voice over the phone. (I'm not kidding. There's science behind this claim.)

Also, remember those messy feelings we discussed earlier? The anger, fear, and resentment? You have to face those and deal with them before going into an interview. They will only get in the way of you showing up as your very best self. And you deserve that—the chance to show up as your best self.

6. Be an encouraging and a positive force when you network

We all have bad days. All of us. That said, when you go out to network, do your best to be open and helpful to others. I guarantee you'll feel 100% better at the end of the networking event if you put yourself out there as a positive and encouraging force, instead of as someone who just complained about how tough it is in the marketplace.

What you focus on expands. (Wayne Dyer, Ph.D.) Focus on what you want your future to look like and what you can do *right now* to move yourself into that future. And if you help someone else in the meantime, you'll leave the event stronger and more uplifted yourself. I know that helping others when you're needing help yourself may seem counterintuitive, but trust me, it works. What goes around comes around.

7. Get an accountability partner—not your significant other

We can all benefit from an accountability partner.

Who an accountability partner *is not*:

- It is *not* your spouse or significant other. If you're unemployed, that person is under stress, too. A discussion between two stressed people about what is and is not working about the day's job seeking activity can go downhill rather quickly.
- It is *not* someone who blames or shames you about what you did or did not get done in the interim.

Who an accountability partner *is*:

- A fellow job seeker who understands what you're going through.
- A colleague or friend who has been in your shoes.
- Someone who can listen without judgment.
- Someone who can celebrate with you when you make headway.
- Someone with whom you can discuss possible next steps.
- Someone you will contact to report on your progress.

> **Tip:** Always put the burden of contact on yourself. Never put the other person in the position of calling to monitor or nag you. And make sure you contact that person in the way that is most convenient for *them* (email, text, phone?).

There have been times when I made a call or submitted something on Thursday afternoon at 4:30 PM because I had to tell my accountability partner on Friday morning what action I had or had not taken. It works.

Many of us tend to procrastinate on tasks that we dread or feel uncertain about, so having an accountability partner can help immensely.

We can also use this person to share "what's working" in our job search. Two heads are better than one.

8. Take good physical care of yourself so that you can keep getting out there

Taking care of yourself mentally, physically, and emotionally during your job transition is not optional. It is a must.

Being unemployed is not for the faint of heart. Keeping yourself mentally, emotionally, and physically fit takes work.

These tips will help:

- **Good sleep:** You can't afford to be sleep-deprived now. It's not pretty what that does to your brain chemistry, and you're going to need all the good molecules you can get to help your brain function healthily during your job transition.
- **Exercise:** This is not just for your physical health. This is also for your brain and emotional health. Exercising creates serotonin, which helps with a positive attitude. It also gets more oxygen to your brain cells. Your brain consumes more oxygen than any other organ in your body. So while you're helping keep the pounds off and getting those muscles strong and toned, you're also getting more oxygen to your brain. Exercise is something you can't afford *not* to do.
- **Stay healthy in general:** Don't ignore your eating habits or become sedentary. Don't stay up late and miss out on good sleep. A job transition can be a very stressful experience. You're going to need your strength.
  - Less caffeine, more water
  - Less television, more moderate exercise like daily walking
  - Less sugar, more fruits and vegetables and lean protein

At the risk of sounding overly parental here, your immune system is challenged enough by the sheer stress of the job hunt. Give yourself a break. Take good care of yourself physically. Soapbox off.

9. Keep your spirits up, mind your attitude

Are you familiar with the phrase "garbage in, garbage out"? It really applies here. Consciously choose positive input from sources you can trust to be uplifting. If you allow yourself to dwell on "how bad it is out there" and listen to grumblers and naysayers, guess what your mind is going to be filled with? You cannot afford those negative thoughts. It's not pretty, it doesn't feel good, and it doesn't help you accomplish what you need to.

Not everyone who loves you can be the uplifting force that you need right now. Spend your time with people who can help you move forward by focusing on the positive. Forgive the people in your life who cannot be this way for you; love them anyway. But choose to seek out those who know how to be encouraging.

Choose positive books and tapes to read and listen to. Different kinds of books appeal to different people. I've listed both spiritual and psychological ones in ***Recommended Resources.***

Chapter 2—Are You Introverted or Extraverted and Why It Matters

Why does it matter whether you are introverted or extraverted? Because based on your preference, you will have different challenges during your job search and transition. Introverts and extraverts have different strengths and blind spots, and, therefore, may find different tips helpful for performing at their best.

If you are prone to introversion, read the tips for introverts:

- *Chapter 5—Networking Tips for Introverts*
- *Chapter 3—Taking Care of Yourself during the Job Search*
- *Chapter 8—Interview Tips for Introverts*

For introverted Boomers, in particular, you've probably been in the workforce a good while. If you are primarily introverted, you've had to develop some extraverted parts of yourself to get work done and to survive. So you may feel like more of a mixed bag (introvert and extravert) than you did, say, when you first started working. And that's fine. Read both sets of tips if you'd like—both might be useful for you. But, I would focus on the tips especially for introverts first.

If you are prone to extraversion, read the chapters with tips for extraverts:

- *Chapter 6—Networking Tips for Extraverts*
- *Chapter 3—Taking Care of Yourself during the Job Search*
- *Chapter 9—Interview Tips for Extraverts*

For extraverted Boomers, in particular, you've probably been in the workforce a good while. If you're primarily extraverted, your work probably did not bring out the introverted parts of you, because extraverts are so rewarded in the workplace, as a general rule. That said, life has probably helped you develop the introverted side of yourself, so you may feel like more of a mixed bag than you did in your 20s. If that's the case, both sets of tips might be useful to you. But I would focus on the tips especially for extraverts first.

If you don't know where you fall or you fall somewhere in between, then consider the tips for both introverts and extraverts, and take what is useful to you from each. You may find using the mini-instrument below helpful as you consider your preferences. Whatever the results though, your preferences are what *you* decide they are.

To Help Determine Your Preference

In each row, put a check in the column that best describes you—A or B. If both columns describe you, no problem; just check the box in both columns.

What Recharges Your Batteries?

A	B
☐ Talking things over with a group	☐ Taking time alone to collect your thoughts
☐ Saying things out loud so you can figure out what you think	☐ Getting information ahead of time so you can think things through before you speak
☐ Meeting new people	☐ Spending time with 1 or 2 friends
☐ Working with a team, brainstorming	☐ Having some quiet time alone after going to a meeting

Which Best Describes Your Behavior?

A	B
☐ You tend to find being in a group energizing.	☐ You like people, but after a while, being with a group is draining.
☐ You tend to "think out loud."	☐ You think before you speak and use few words.
☐ You prefer to bounce ideas off other people instead of thinking in your office alone.	☐ You would speak up more often in meetings if you felt like you could "get a word in edgewise."
☐ You tend to think that silence means agreement.	☐ You believe that silence can mean many things.
☐ In a group, you tend to speak to fill the silence.	☐ Being alone, after being with a group, recharges your batteries.
☐ You tend to speak off the cuff.	☐ You like to get information ahead of time so that you can think about it before you have to talk about it.

TOTAL: A= ___   B= ___

> **Results:** If you have more checks in column A, your preference might be for extraversion. In that case, focus on the extraverted tips in the chapters recommended above. If you have more checks in column B, your preference might be for introversion, so focus on the tips for introverts. If the totals are close, consider reading both sets of tips and use what is most helpful to you in each.

Do I have to be one or the other?

Remember, no one is completely introverted or completely extraverted. We all extravert some mental functions and introvert others. That said, this preference is not necessarily a toggle switch for you—either/or, on/off. Instead, you may fall somewhere along the spectrum, leaning more heavily toward either extraversion or introversion.

And there's no right or wrong place to fall along the spectrum. Wherever your preferences fall is just fine. It's just helpful to know where you fall on the spectrum so that you can manage your preferences in the appropriate circumstances and show up wherever you go as your best self. For example, sometimes an extravert may need to hold back a bit to allow others to have "air time" in the group discussion. Or an introvert may need to summon the energy to enter the conversation and share when they otherwise might not be inclined to speak up.

As Dr. Otto Kroeger, famous expert, speaker, and author of many books in the field of psychological type, said:[1]

> **"I'm not asking you *not to be who you are*.**
> **I'm just asking you *to manage it better."***

We all have preferences, so we all have things it would behoove us to manage at times.

A Personal Example: Managing my Extraverted Self

As a real-world example, I realize I'm clearly extraverted in my preferences. When I teach a room full of computer software engineers, I know that their preferences are very different from mine. Their preference for introversion may be anywhere from moderate to very clear, and the percentage of introverts in that room may be as high as 83%. (I know this from actual data from my IT clients.)

I will not be helpful to them if I show up as my unabashed extraverted self. I need to adjust in order to be more effective. I need to rein in my energy, dial down my expressiveness somewhat, and slow down my pace. I also need to do small-table discussions instead of whole-room

---

1   I had the pleasure of hearing Otto say this in person at an APTi (Assoc. of Psychological Type Int'l) conference, one of the many times I heard him speak over the years. I was so struck by it that I've never forgotten it. Otto made incredible contributions to the field of psychological type before passing away in the summer of 2013.

discussions.

Not that there's anything *wrong* with that. There's nothing inherently wrong with my more usual style and process. But if I want to be effective, I'll reel it in so that I can better connect with these particular clients and create a learning environment that helps meet their needs. No good or bad here. Just adjusting to be more effective with the people actually in the room with me that day.

One IT manager attended my team training twice, one year apart—once with managers and directors and later with his own employees. He wrote on his evaluation at the later training, "Carol seems to have reined in her extraversion." He meant it as a compliment, and I took it as one. It literally helped his learning style and that of his employees for me to make this adjustment for them.

Chapter 3—Taking Care of Yourself during the Job Search

Why Taking Care of Yourself Matters

This may not be where you think you need to start. You may be eager to move on to resumes and interviews and networking. These three things are important. But taking care of yourself is just as important as taking care of these other things. If you fall into healthy habits now, at the beginning, your job transition will be easier.

Learning to take care of yourself during this process might be the most important thing you can learn to do first.

You are your instrument and you are the product you are selling.

You need to be in good shape to make good decisions and present your best self.

Whether your job search period is a sprint or a marathon, you will help yourself right off the starting line by accepting the fact that this time—while exciting and even energizing—can also be challenging and you will need support and self-care to make it through with grace.

We're going to cover some very basic things you can do to take care of yourself during this transition, so that you can

- stay healthy.
- manage your challenging feelings without getting stuck in them.
- show up as your best self in an interview.
- be an encouraging and a positive force when you network.
- keep up your spirits and energy level so that you can keep getting out there!

Introvert or Extravert and Why It Matters

Introverts and extraverts can have very different needs and potential pitfalls during times of stress and transition. Look for the specially marked sections for your preference in these tips.

Top 9 Recommendations

In my three years working with a local job seekers' networking group, I have learned much from both my introverted and extraverted clients and would like to thank them all for contributing to this list of tips. I have spent countless hours field-testing these recommendations with students in my classroom at a local community college and with job seekers in the networking group that I facilitate. I am convinced they will help you through your own job search.

1. Balance your needs for down time and connecting with others.
2. Get the support you need and deserve.
3. Get up and get dressed!
4. Structure your days and record what you accomplish.
5. Attend networking groups—it's essential.
6. Have an accountability partner.
7. Exercise!
8. Help someone else.
9. Volunteer.

Recommendation 1: Balance your needs for down time and connecting with others.

Introverts: Get the necessary down time you need to recharge. Introverts recharge their batteries when it's quiet, they're alone, and they have time to think things through. This is a physiological need. It's not an excuse; it's real. So honor that need in you!

The job transition period can be very stressful, and you may feel even more need for alone time than under normal conditions. Give yourself that time. It's healing. Also, don't hesitate to ask your loved ones for the alone time you need. Help them understand that it has nothing to do with them; it's about you and your need to recharge your batteries during a difficult time.

Extraverts: You need external stimulation. Don't "hole up" in your house. Extraverts need more dopamine hits in their brains than introverts do. In fact, the same amount of dopamine that makes an extravert feel alert, alive, and engaged can make an introvert feel overstimulated and exhausted in a very short amount of time.

This need is physiological and real; you have to honor it. When I go to a café to work on my writing, I imagine that a lot of the other folks camped out there with their computers are extraverts who seem to understand that they just can't stay in the house all day.

And they're right. If something as small as leaving the house can keep your brain in a happier state, then it would be silly not to do it. (I'm currently editing this in the Mad Hatter Café and Bakery. What's good for the goose is good for the gander.)

Recommendation 2: Get the support you need—and deserve.

Introverts: Reach out to others. Do not go through this alone. While, as an introvert, you don't need as much stimulation from the environment as extraverts do, retreating, which is probably your first instinct here, is not helpful. Nor is it helpful to go to so many events that you exhaust yourself. You need down time to recharge your batteries, but you should not retreat and become a recluse. It's a delicate balance for introverts, so just be aware that you need to balance the need for reaching out for support from others with your very real need for down time.

Extraverts: You usually don't need to be told to "reach out to others" because you naturally tend to engage with the external world. But admitting to someone that you're out of work and could use their help is another matter entirely. Even extraverts can have a tendency to withdraw under pressure and stress. You find yourself unwilling to admit that you're even looking for work or—even more vulnerable—that you're having an awful day. Beware this tendency to withdraw under stress. Talk about what you're going through with someone you can trust with this level of personal disclosure.

Everyone: You owe it to yourself to choose your supporters carefully. While there may be many people in your life who love you and would do their best to help you, not all of them may have the skill to respond in a way that is beneficial to you.

Friends and family members often think they're helping by saying things like, "You still don't have another job?" "Maybe you're not trying hard enough." Or "I'm not worried about you; you'll be fine." Try not to judge them, but do the right thing for yourself and choose confidants who can be constructive and supportive in a way that lifts you up and moves you forward.

Pick supporters who, as researcher and author Brené Brown would say, "have earned the right to hear your story."

Recommendation 3: Get up and get dressed. (I'm not kidding.)

One morning about four months into my 2008 job transition, I was feeling pretty down around 10:30 AM. I called a long-time friend and colleague who'd successfully navigated her way through two layoffs and had landed a job already (she was in the IT industry). I felt that she was safe to call and that she could give me productive advice.

"Jenny," I said, "I'm feeling really bad about things today. Is it okay to just go back to bed and pull the covers over my head?" Without missing a beat, she replied, "Yes, it is. But you may only do that ONE DAY a week."

She made me laugh so hard that it actually pulled me out of my funk. Humor and friends are two great tools for surviving a job transition.

Then she said something that really threw me. "What are you wearing?"

"What?" I replied. Surely I had not heard her correctly.

"What . . . are . . . you . . . wearing??"

"I'm in my pajamas and working at my computer. I'm not going anywhere today."

Then, the real lesson began.

"No, no, no. No sitting around in pajamas or sweats. Get up, get dressed, put on your game face, and get on a schedule."

I have never, ever forgotten her words and I've shared them with countless job seekers since. Sitting around in pajamas or sweats is a set-up for depression. Get up and get ready for your day even if you're not going out. You cannot afford to sit around and fall down the slippery slope of depression. This transition phase is hard enough as it is.

Get up, get dressed, get on a schedule. Meet your day like the adult and professional that you are. (But if you need to pull the covers over your head at some point, you have my personal permission to do that—but only one day per week.)

Recommendation 4: Structure your days and record what you accomplish.

Have a schedule. Provide yourself with the structure you had before you lost the job. You'll be amazed at how fast the week goes by. You'll get to Friday afternoon, knowing you were racing around all week, but still wondering: exactly what did I get done?

Fill in your calendar with your activities, or just keep a daily to-do list. Cross things off as you get them done. Not only does this give you a sense of accomplishment, but it gives you a way to see how you're using your time, and how your time could be better used.

There's also another benefit to filling in your calendar. You may need protection from family members who start asking you to do all sorts of things during the day because "you're not working." But, you are working. You need to remind them of that. Your job is to look for a job. You are not available to run errands for them all day. Your filled-in calendar will demonstrate that.

Recommendation 5: Attend networking groups—it's essential.

Networking groups can provide valuable contacts into an organization.

Over 80% of jobs are obtained through networking.

While no one but you can land you the job you want, someone else can "get eyes on" your resume. There are still so many people out of work that HR professionals and recruiters are overwhelmed. It's not that you're getting rejected so much as you're not getting seen.

At the point of this writing, North Carolina has three job seekers for every one open position. And that isn't counting all of the people who have fallen off the unemployment rolls and just plain given up. Even without this group, the numbers are still mind-boggling.

That's why now, it's more important than ever that you network your way into a company. Find someone who will put your resume in front of someone else. This person may be

- the HR recruiter or hiring manager.
- someone who knows the recruiter or hiring manager or works in the same company and can physically hand them your resume.
- another manager or an executive in the company who is willing to recommend you or simply pass your resume on to the recruiter so that your resume will at least "get eyes on" it.

I have a friend who got an interview, nailed it, and ended up with a six-figure engineering job. She got the job on her own merits, but her resume was *seen* by the HR recruiter because a colleague knew the CEO and emailed her resume to him. Yes, she also went through proper channels. She did submit her resume online through the website. But let's face it, if a resume comes into an HR recruiter's email box from the CEO, it will at least get a once-over. She was well-qualified for the position, proved it, and got the job—but she got the *chance* because someone she met in a networking group helped her "get eyes on" her resume.

That person might be a woman you meet at a professional training (my story) or a neighbor's husband (another colleague's story). These stories are real and happen again and again. Do not underestimate the ability of others to help you "get seen" by the right people.

And try to remember—you should always be on the lookout for someone you can help in return. Pay it forward.

An introvert's biggest danger with networking is feeling overwhelmed walking into a large room full of people. The next danger is to overdo it, exhaust yourself, then stop going altogether. You cannot afford *not* to network. So let me give you two tips:

- **Select your events carefully.** Don't overdo it. Probably no more than two networking events per week. Maybe even just one to start. It's exhausting for an introvert to have to overdo socializing.
- **Let's reframe this whole experience.** You're not walking into a "room full of people." You're walking into a room, and you're going to have a sequence of one-on-one conversations. You can do that. One-on-one is your forte. And when you get tired, just leave. That way, you'll have energy the next time you need to attend a networking event.

An extravert's biggest danger with networking is that they'll do too much of it and not be focused about it. I have to talk introverts into networking. I have to talk extraverts into focusing so that they strategically choose which networking events to attend. If they don't focus, they can easily network so much they don't get other things done. That said, networking is invaluable and it is required, not optional. Do it; just don't overdo it.

Recommendation 6: Get (and be) an accountability partner.

Everyone can benefit from having an accountability partner. Everyone. This is not someone who shames you or wags a finger when you don't get everything done. This is someone who keeps you focused, someone to whom you report your progress and admit your occasional downfalls.

There are all sorts of things that are uncomfortable about the job search process, and we've all been guilty of procrastinating when we don't want to do certain things. Knowing that you have to email your partner, or call them, or face them across a table in a coffee shop on Friday morning can motivate you to do something on Thursday that you otherwise would have put off until Monday.

> **Important Tip: your accountability partner should not be your significant other.**

If you're out of work, your significant other is also under stress! Two stressed people discussing the ups and downs of the job hunt may not be a productive experience. Use another job-seeking colleague as your accountability partner and do the same thing in return.

One of my workshops was half-filled one month by "an accountability group" of four women who had met in another workshop. (Our local community college offers incredible classes to the unemployed!) They met every Friday morning to discuss how the job search had gone, what had worked, what hadn't, what they were going to try next and commit to for next weekend. You'll be amazed at the powerful things this kind of duo or even group can do to energize your job search and keep you going.

Remember: the point is not to meet to kvetch. Fess up to what didn't work, console each other on those things, celebrate what things did help you move forward, and commit to what you'll do for next week. Share best practices and help each other land even faster.

Recommendation 7: Exercise!

There are at least two reasons to make yourself exercise during this crucial and stressful time:

- **It creates serotonin in your brain and that protects you from depression.** Studies have shown that exercising moderately three to four times a week for 30 minutes is as effective as some prescription anti-depressants in relieving depression.
- **It provides your brain with more oxygen.** Did you know that your brain is the largest consumer of oxygen in your body? So you're not just benefiting your muscles when you exercise. Your brain is benefiting from the additional oxygen in your bloodstream too.

It's a win/win. Seriously, you can't afford not to exercise.

Recommendation 8: Volunteer!

Volunteering accomplishes multiple things, all of which are to your benefit.

Four quick benefits are:

1. You need some way to answer the question, "What have you been doing since the layoff?" Now, we all know that looking for a job is a full-time job in itself (actually, it's more time-consuming than a full-time job), but you can't say that. Well, you can say that, but it's frowned upon.
2. Volunteering demonstrates that you're not sitting around eating bon-bons.
3. It shows you're civic-minded, and that's a good thing.
4. It keeps your skill set up to date.

Continue to use and update your skills: Through volunteering, you can actually benefit an organization you really believe in, one that will uplift you and help you continue to use your skill set and prove that you're staying active during your job transition.

Non-profit organizations don't just need people to lick envelopes. Now, more than ever, they need people with professional skills to volunteer help in specialized areas. Help with their website, help with fundraising, do an IT project they need but have no budget for. Help the board accomplish a project they don't have staff to accomplish but would love to get done for the people they serve. With non-profits hurting for funding, you can be part of the answer for them. And they can be part of the answer for you, too—helping you prove that your skills are still up to date and that you are a productive member of society with something valuable to offer.

Recommendation 9: Help someone else.

As Anthony Robbins, the famous self-improvement guru, points out, it is absolutely impossible to feel sorry for yourself when you are helping someone else. Giving and receiving turn out to be the same thing. When you help someone else, it lifts your self-esteem and sense of empowerment all at the same time. Win/win. Why would we not do this?

I'll tell you why: we're under incredible stress and it feels like we couldn't possibly take on one more thing.

While it's true that we can seem too overwhelmed to take on one more thing, helping someone else maybe the very thing we need to do. By focusing on someone other than ourselves and on someone else's issue, we stop, for a small while, from focusing so much on our own. Then a funny thing happens. We realize we are capable and that we can make a difference.

We just have to be willing to pull ourselves out of our own myopic concern, even if just for a few minutes, to focus on something we can to do help someone else. All of us can do this. And everyone involved benefits.

Chapter 4—Networking: It's for All of Us Now

"The Facts, Ma'am, Just the Facts"

Fact: Networking is necessary in the 21st century job market.

Go ahead and get your resistance out of the way and accept this now. Networking is not just for sales people or executives any more. It's for all of us. Sending your resumes and applications into the great vortex of the Internet is not going to cut it. You have to back up job applications with networking your way into a company to get the opportunity to "get eyes on" your resume.

You're not being rejected.
You're often not even being seen.

"Getting eyes on it" is the key strategy.
Networking can do that.

Fact: Our jobs will be shorter and we'll be between jobs more often.

We are all going to have more jobs for shorter periods of time. Just burrowing into one company and trying to make it up that famous ladder, with few connections to the outside world, is no longer a successful long-term strategy for most people.

If we want *between-job* periods to be less economically devastating to our finances, we're going to have to learn to stay networked and make our way with agility into that next contract (a "soft landing") or real job with benefits (a "hard landing").

Fact: Over 80% of jobs are acquired through networking.

I know it's easier to just stay at home and enter applications through the Internet all day. But the data shows that getting out there and networking improves your chances of turning an application into an interview and then into a job landing. As tempting as it is to stay at home, can you really afford to avoid an activity that leads to over 80% of job landings?

Tips for pioneering this brave new world of networking

Tip 1: Check your attitude at the door—how can I add value to others?

Whatever happens next, the evening cannot be a loss if you walk into the event with the attitude, "How can I be helpful to someone here?" You can't go wrong with that positive, helpful attitude. It will put you in the right mind frame. You'll be actively listening for an opportunity to connect them with something or someone who can help. A Giver mentality is a magnet to the right connections; an obvious Taker mentality can be a real turn-off and prevent you from making beneficial connections. Be a Giver first. Pay it forward.

Tip 2: Fewer deep connections are worth more than many shallow ones.

You don't have to meet everyone in the room. If you make one or two real connections at an event, you're doing great.

Shallow connections don't mean much and don't get you much. Meeting fewer people but connecting in a way that helps build a relationship is your best strategy in the long run.

And by "connecting," I don't mean you've met your new best friend. I mean that your conversation was meaningful enough that they'll really remember you and something important about you. It's especially important that you help them associate your name and face with the kind of job you are seeking. You want them to think of you when they see a listing or hear of a yet-unlisted opening that would be perfect for you. And if you went in with the right attitude, they'll remember that you seemed like a Giver, a helpful person, not a Taker. And they'll be more inclined to help you in the future. (I just heard a report on NPR the other day about recent research on this.) Being a Taker is a short-term solution. We all need long-term strategies, not short-term solutions.

Tip 3: You never know where that next valuable connection is coming from.

Choose your events with care, but be careful not to pre-judge people. And do not assume that the next great connection is going to come from your friend of 20 years. That's not how it happens.

The next person who gets your resume to the right place or who knows a name for you is probably not your best friend. It may be your neighbor's husband who's willing to walk your resume into the office after you've applied online. It may be someone you worked with 10 years ago that you just reconnected with on LinkedIn. Or it may be someone you connected with at an event last week who's out there paying it forward like you are. There's no "tit for tat" in this equation. But, what goes around comes around. Be out there, be helpful. Your turn will come.

Your particular challenges about networking?

Introverts and extraverts have different challenges with networking. Introverts tend to think that they are the only ones challenged by networking. It's not true. Extraverts are challenged, too—just in a different way. For tips on how to handle your particular challenges, see *Chapter 5—Networking Tips for Introverts* or *Chapter 6—Networking Tips for Extraverts*.

Opportunities to Network

1. **Job seekers networking groups** can take many forms. In the area where I live, most are held in churches, even if the church itself does not run them. Usually church members or other non-profit groups such as Step-Up Ministries run them. Google "job seekers" for your area. Also, ask around. I found both of my main groups by word of mouth. Once there, I was able to get a listing of many more in the area that I hadn't heard of. Most are run by volunteers who regularly donate their time to help job seekers connect with each other, hear speakers address different topics, and find classes where they can learn about useful job seeking skills and tools—such as how to rewrite your resumes, get practice interviewing, and get job leads.

2. **Professional meetings** related to your field (such as engineering, web design, training, IT) are great sources of information and opportunities to connect with others in your chosen field or a field that you want to move into. I attend three different groups that are integral to the kind of work I do: ATD (for trainers and curriculum designers), APTI (for psychological type professionals), and TODN (for organization development professionals). I highly recommend staying in touch with your fellow professionals or getting to know local professionals in a field you want to move into. They may know about openings before they're posted anywhere.

3. **Professional trainings** are offered by local chapters of professional organizations, as well as community colleges and continuing education centers at local universities. Attending such events can both keep you in touch with folks in your field—even introduce you to new ones—and help you keep your skills up to date. Employers can be squeamish about job candidates who have been unemployed for over six months. While we all know that's an unreasonable expectation in this economic environment, we can't change their attitudes. What you can do is show that you're keeping your skills up to date.

4. **Job fairs** can provide good opportunities to talk to recruiters at companies with current job openings. Job fairs can also be highly specialized, which is good for you when your specialty is the focus of the job fair. Go to a few to get the feel of them, but learn to choose carefully so that you're investing your time wisely.

5. **Meetups** abound and can come in many shapes and sizes. Even if the Meetup is focused on a hobby instead of a career field, you might meet someone who has helpful information for you and vice versa. Meetups aren't just for hobbies anymore, though. There are more and more listings for groups that are connected to job-related areas of interest. Google "Meetups" for your local area.

Chapter 5—Networking Tips for Introverts

Here are my top six networking challenges for introverted job seekers. I've field-tested these for six months in my *pro bono* work as a facilitator at a local job seekers' networking group. I'd like to thank all of my introverted clients who continue to validate and contribute solidly to the value of this list. I'd also like to thank Consultant Heather Hollick for contributing to my understanding of networking challenges for introverts.

Top 6 Networking Challenges for Introverts and What to Do about Them

Challenge 1: Networking events are overwhelming at times.

First, you should know that extraverts can find these events overwhelming, too. You are not alone in this. That said, you will find them depleting before the typical extravert does, so take care of yourself both before and afterward. Make sure you get plenty of down time earlier that day and again afterward so that you can recharge your batteries.

Honor your natural sense of what's enough and what's too much. Pick your events strategically so that you use your energy wisely. It's quality—not volume—that counts. While we all need to be strategic in use of our time, this is not quite as important for extraverts as introverts. For one thing, many extraverts are recharging their batteries while they're in that noisy room full of people. It's not draining to them. That said, even extraverts will do better to choose strategically which networking events they attend.

Leave before you feel depleted. If you force yourself to stay after your energy is gone, you won't accomplish anything and you'll dread going to the next one. Give yourself permission to leave when it's right for you, so that you'll have the energy and will to go back—either to that same event or a different one.

In the future, more and more of us will either work independently or change jobs more frequently. We need to keep our networks up and running so that we can use them to get the next job with a shorter period of downtime.

Networking will not stop after you land a job, so find a way that works for you. It's important to do networking in a way that works for you because networking should not stop after you get re-employed. Oh, the frequency of networking events you attend will probably go down once you get re-employed, but there is no going back in time. We are all going to be living in a more networked world, and introverts need to have a plan that lets them engage without being depleted.

Challenge 2: Chitchat is hard.

Admittedly, chitchat is easy for some and downright painful for others. Let's come up with a few options here so instead of feeling at a loss, you will have a multiple-choice list to pick from.

- ☐ **"Hi, I'm <name>. <Extend your hand.>What are you working on?" or "What brings you here?"** Great ice-breaker, no meaningless banter required. Also, you're inviting them to talk about themselves immediately. It's all good.[1]

- ☐ **"Hi, I'm <name>. <Extend your hand.>This is my first time in this venue. What do you like about coming to this event?"** Always ask an open question instead of a closed one. A closed question invites a very brief answer, such as "yes" or "no," and does not further the conversation or get the other person to open up and engage with you. An open question moves the conversation forward and invites the other person to enter and contribute real content. For example, it's the dif-

---

[1] Thanks to Heather Hollick, speaker, coach, and networking expert for this great tip for introverted networkers. Heather is living proof that introverts can network very effectively. See www.HeatherHollick.com.

ference between "Do you like?" and "What do you like about . . .?" The second question could start an interesting conversation. The first one just puts the ball immediately back in your court.

- ☐ **"Hi, I'm <name>. <Extend your hand.> My spouse and I just relocated here from <location>. We have grandchildren here. Have you been here long?"** You've given them multiple opportunities to take you up on some topic: where you used to live, tips for someone new, grandkids. Whatever the content, this kind of start gives you multiple possibilities.

I'd love to make this list longer. Email me with ice-breaker questions that you, as an introvert, have used that were comfortable and worked well to start a conversation: info@effectivewithpeople.com.

Challenge 3: I can't get a word in edgewise.

> **Understand that an extravert's sense of time is different from yours.** They keep talking because you're not. The silence you're comfortable with is strained for them. The pause you need before you enter makes them think they need to speak again.
>
> **Take a breath, raise your energy, and jump in** there more quickly than is natural for you. Often an extravert is genuinely relieved that you've finally come out to engage.

Here's a true story from an introverted business owner who attended one of my talks at a local city club. The next week I ran into her at a chamber event and she was very excited. "Carol, I met with a potential customer last Friday. I was really hoping to sign him up. But he kept talking and talking, and then I remembered what you said: 'He's never going to stop talking. He's waiting for me to *jump in.*' So I did. And it *worked*. His face actually looked relieved when I finally spoke up. The conversation flowed great from that point, and the outcome was a success. I did sign him up."

I realize that at networking you're not trying to "sign up a customer," but you are trying to get a conversation off the ground to see if you have anything in common to pursue together or if you can be helpful to each other. The first time you do this—just jump in and be rewarded by the visible relief on the extravert's face—the easier it will be the next time. You'll be a believer.

Challenge 4: Why don't they realize I'm listening and engaged?

Without signals from you, extraverts think you're not "with them." Remember that extraverts have a dramatically different sense of time than you do. Give them what they need: a verbal or even a visual cue, such as a change in your facial expression, that shows you're listening and engaged. Introverts can have incredibly still faces. (As an expressive extravert, I stand in amazement at their facial stillness and control.) It's actually a sign that you're focusing and listening. The problem is that extraverts can't "see" your engagement unless you give them a visual or auditory clue. One introverted client, when asked a question, would literally tilt her head and say "hmm" to show that she was thinking about her answer. Extraverts did not tend to interrupt her because they got the signal.

Challenge 5: Sometimes I don't think of what I wish I'd said until the next day.

The "time to mull" factor: I cannot tell you how many times an introverted client has said to me, "I think of what I wish I'd said—the next day <audible sigh>." This is a common phenomenon. You are not alone. Introverts need time to internally process before they know how they want to respond. If they've already been thinking about it, sure, they can answer more quickly. But if they haven't, they don't tend to have a ready answer. You should use this phenomenon to your advantage. It's a genuine opportunity to reconnect later in email or LinkedIn.

Great opportunity to reconnect: You don't have to invent some flimsy excuse to reconnect in a follow-up email. You have a genuine reason. On the very next day, you can send an email that reads, "Hey, I was thinking about what you said, and I remembered this article I thought you'd be interested in. . ." Or, "I was thinking of what you said and it occurred to me that . . ." An excuse to reconnect is a good thing; use it. And the fact that you were still thinking of something they said 24 hours later is a compliment to them. You just can't lose with this one.

Remember to get their card: If you didn't get their card, reconnecting will be harder. You'll have to remember the correct spelling of the person's name and hope they're in LinkedIn to make reconnecting possible.

In one sense it doesn't matter how many cards you give out. You have no control over what happens to those cards. The ones you do have control over are the cards that *you* asked for and leave with. Are you going to use them to connect? Reconnect? (Or will they just lay in that drawer, with all the others that didn't get follow-ups either?)

Make a conscious choice; reconnect with purpose and add value for the other person whenever you can.

Challenge 6: How to avoid "deer in the headlights" experiences?

Prepare, prepare, prepare: The more prepared you are, the fewer "deer in headlights" experiences you'll have. I know that sounds embarrassingly simple, but to a large extent it's really, really true.

Toss the question back their way: The stakes are less high here than in an interview, so you can experiment some if you like. If you find a question surprising, you can say that. "That's an interesting question. I've never really thought of it that way. What are your thoughts?" Seriously, what do you have to lose? You could end up starting an interesting conversation.

Or you could say, "That's an interesting question. I'd have to mull over that. What are your thoughts?"

An old stand-by: Then there's the well-established way to buy time to think. Just repeat the question, as though you're restating it for clarity. My mother used this on me my entire extraverted childhood. Trust me. It worked for her. She got more information out of me and she bought herself time to consider if she wanted to say yes or not. Smart woman, my introverted mother.

Chapter 6—Networking Tips for Extraverts

Here are my top six networking challenges for extraverted job seekers. I've field-tested these for six months as a facilitator at a local job seekers' networking group. I'd like to thank all of my extraverted clients who have validated and who continue to contribute solidly to the value of this list.

Top 6 Networking Challenges for Extraverts and What to Do About Them

Challenge 1: I was just "thinking out loud."

> **Beware your natural "thinking out loud" processing style.** In conversations, this can mean that you take up more than your fair share of air time. Think about how that can come across at a networking event. It can make you look self-absorbed or seem that you have no interest in what the other person has to contribute. It can also come across as, well, arrogant—unkind, I know, but it can happen. Just be aware and rein in your tendency to process everything out loud.
>
> **How Introverts do it differently: they edit before they speak.** One of the reasons extraverts and introverts have such a natural difficulty with timing is that extraverts tend to quite literally "think out loud." Introverts, on the other hand, mentally retrieve information from their frontal lobes, edit their words, and then speak. All of that internal processing takes more time than it does for you to think out loud. Give them that time.
>
> If you don't, you become the "I couldn't get a word in edgewise with that guy" guy. You don't want to be that guy. Pause. Breathe. It will seem like an eternity at times, but try to manage your oh-so-natural impulse to jump back in.

You will be richly rewarded when you accomplish a real connection with an introverted colleague instead of walking away from one who thinks you're just another extravert who talks to hear himself talk. All it takes is self-management and an understanding that the introvert is probably thinking about how to reply to you. It's all happening on the inside with an introvert.

Challenge 2: Why don't the introverts just jump in and speak up?

Get comfortable with longer pauses and more silence. Introverts aren't jumping in because you're never pausing long enough to let them enter the conversation. Introverts can have a profoundly different sense of time than extraverts; they truly need more time to reply than you do.

This is one of those tips that falls into the "not difficult, just really, really hard" category. This difference between introverts and extraverts can be so natural and so "wired in" that it takes real effort to overcome it and compensate appropriately. It's not difficult to do it the new way, it's just really, really hard to *remember* to think and choose the new behavior.

Seriously, you will need to manage that pressure inside your chest that is saying, "They didn't understand. They must need me to restate the question. I must need to say something else—NOW." No, they don't need you to restate anything. They need you to be quiet and let them think and process in order to give you a thoughtful reply.

Remember to pause and invite the other person to share their perspective. Introverts don't tend to just jump in. Invite them in. I know, I know, *you* don't need to be invited in, but everyone isn't you. I can't tell you how shocked I was when I learned in my psychological type qualification training that some people don't interject themselves until they're invited.

As astonished as I was at that fact—being a flaming extravert myself—I tried it and it actually worked. It truly did get the more introverted person into the conversation with me.

I decided to try it out the week I returned from my qualifications training. I sat down to lunch with a friend who is a professional writer and a published poet. Instead of doing most of the talking as I usually do, I asked him a question. He paused, thought, then responded. After another bite or two, I asked another question. Twenty minutes later, mid-raised forkful of food, he looked down at my empty lunch plate, then at his still half-full plate, and said, "Well, I guess I had something to say today." *No*, I thought but did not say aloud, *your extraverted friend just learned how to be a better friend to you today.*

As odd as this may sound, we may actually come across as rude by not pausing to invite introverts into the conversation. Extraverts don't mean it as rude. It would simply never occur to us. Just another lesson, I suppose, in how dead wrong we can be when we make assumptions about others based on our own natural, yet unconscious, preferences.

Challenge 3: I'm uncomfortable during silences. I just have to speak and fill them up.

Avoid the tendency to fill in the silences. Introverts seem to understand that silences are okay; extraverts tend to feel uncomfortable in them and fill them up with talking, making it difficult for the introvert to enter the conversation and engage with them.

Don't let yourself talk your way out of the job or the connection. I can't tell you how many times an extravert has said to me, "I have listened to myself talk my way out of getting the job during an interview. I just couldn't make my mouth stop." A networking situation is not always as directly linked to "getting the job," but it might be. Networking can invite the same unconscious behavior on the part of an extravert as an interview does: talking to fill up the empty air time. Because over 80% of jobs are found through networking, do not underestimate how important making a good impression and a real connection at a networking event might be.

Again, if you're an extravert, you're fighting your natural "wiring" to overcome this challenge. It's worth the battle within to do this for yourself. A blown networking interaction could easily translate into a lost opportunity to connect to a future job.

Challenge 4: I seem to talk a lot faster than others.

Slow down. Fast-paced speaking can be energizing and entertaining at times, but during networking it can kill rapport. Extraverts tend to speak more quickly than introverts. Introverts need more processing time than you do because they do more internal processing naturally. Remember: for introverts, it's all happening on the inside.

It's not that they're "dumber" than you or that they don't think as quickly. They just think more before they speak. Your fast-paced talking interferes with their more internal processing style. What will they probably do when faced with your energetic pace? The least painful option is simply to excuse themselves from the conversation as soon as they politely can. This will not help you to widen your network.

How managing this can be a win for you: NLP (neurolinguistic programming) has been around so long that I probably don't need to explain this, but, as an example, matching the other person's pace, or at least coming closer to it, helps the other person feel more comfortable with you and connect. You're fighting your "wiring" on this but you can do it.

Challenge 5: Sometimes I jump in very quickly.

Do not interrupt or talk over someone. Sometimes extraverts jump in very quickly, even overlapping others slightly. Often, it's from enthusiasm and actually indicates that you, the extravert, are feeling in rapport and connecting. Even though the true source is enthusiasm, it can come across as rude to an introvert or even, at times, to another extravert. So beware the "jumping in" tendency.

Male and female culture can be profoundly different on this point. Women tend to use overlapping to show enthusiasm and build rapport with each other. Men can interpret it as trying to take the power in the conversation.

If the other person is more introverted than you are, whether male or female, you can come across as rude or immature or impatient. None of those adjectives will buy you more time with that person or consideration for helping you in the future.

Remember: use the Platinum Rule, not the Golden Rule, especially when considering the differences between extraverts and introverts. The Golden Rule says to treat others as you would like to be treated. Keeping the wide range of natural personality type preferences in mind, instead use the Platinum Rule and treat them as *they* prefer to be treated.

Challenge 6: It's hard not to show it when I know what I want to say.

Listen before you react. Do not open your mouth and set your face, like you're about to dive into the answer. This one ever-so-common behavior of extraverts can have a very negative impact. The most frequent response I get from clients on this point is, "My wife tells me that *all the time*."

The worst thing about this behavior is that it comes across as "You're not even listening to me anymore. What's the point in my finishing my sentence?" If you think about that for a second, you can understand how rapport-killing this seemingly innocent behavior can be.

The sad thing is that, as a fellow extravert, *I know* you may be doing this because you're fully engaged. Yet it's commonly interpreted to mean that you're no longer listening or, perhaps even worse, not serious enough to give your answer some real thought before launching into a response.

Your spouse and your mother may always be annoyed by this, but they love you anyway. John and Jane Doe networker may not love you so much. Rein in that facial expression that says, "I know what I want to say to you *right now.*" Just rein it in. You will benefit from it and so will your current and new relationships.

Chapter 7 — Resumes

Purpose

This is not a "how to do your resume" chapter. This is solid advice on what to expect when creating or updating your resume and where to go to get what you need.

Tip 1: Don't try to do it alone.

- **Use outplacement services.** If your former employer offers outplacement services, use them! They're especially helpful with your resume. Sometimes there is a limitation on how long you have access to those services, so take advantage of them right away. I've spoken with job seekers who were in such a state of shock and/or denial that they waited too long to engage with the services and lost all access to them.

- **Take classes at your local community college.** Many community colleges offer low-cost or no-cost classes on all sorts of topics for job seekers, including classes on constructing your resume.

- **Use a professional career counselor.** If you have the money to hire one, a good professional career counselor can coach your thought process and create a resume that truly reflects your strengths and expertise. Contact me through my website. I'm glad to recommend counselors that I have great confidence in. See www.effectivewithpeople.com.

- **There are tons of books out there.** Look for the ones that have gotten lots of stars from reviewers. Also see ***Recommended Resources*** where I list the books recommended by experienced career counselors.

- **Get input from people who really know you and your work.** We are often blind to our own strengths and skills. Our strengths are so integral to who we are, and how we interface with the world each day, that we're often unconscious of them until someone points them out. Some things can come so naturally and be so easy that you're unaware it's a strength at all. Your colleagues will know your strengths, however, and know the unique skills you bring to the job.

Carefully pick a few people you trust and who really got a chance to see you in action at work or see the quality of your results at work. Send them an email. "Hey, I'm doing my resume and I'd really appreciate the benefit of your perspective. If you had to pick, what would you say were my top three strengths? Please think of behaviors or results I achieved that you know I should lead with when I need to show new potential employers what value I bring to the table. Thanks for taking the time to provide me with feedback."

Tip 2: Expect the frustration of multiple opinions.

Your experience may be that almost every resume expert seems to give you *different* advice. This is an ongoing frustration for job seekers I've worked with. What are you supposed to do with all of the contradictory incoming advice if even the so-called experts can't agree?

First, note patterns in the advice you're given. There will be some common themes. Pay attention to those. Then make the best decision you can based on how well the advice aligns with what you know about your field.

Tip 3: Your resume documents the value you bring to the table; it's a record of *results*, not just a list of *activities*.

The standard resume used to list your job title, company, years of service, and duties performed. Those days are over. Even if you still use a chronological resume, which is fine if that works for you, you should try to steer clear of simply listing your job duties. Companies today are looking for *results* and *accomplishments*—not just activities.

State Results	Instead of Job Duties
• Coached my staff to an increase in 20% sales over 6 months	• Managed staff of 6 sales associates
• Led research team of 12 whose results led to a $6.5 million grant for further research	• Managed research team of 12 researchers

Tip 4: For Boomers: Do not include more than 15+ years of experience.

Here's the logic in this. No, it's not lying. Potential employers can go to LinkedIn, see when you graduated from college, and guess your age range. The point in the resume is to *not give them a reason to exclude you*. If they see 20, 25, 30 years of experience on the resume, chances are they will exclude you based on that alone.

The purpose of your resume is to land the interview, where you will have an opportunity to show the potential employer that your experience is an asset!

Listing less of your job history on your resume will help you get past the age bias and closer to the interview, where you can be considered for the job you deserve.

Tip 5: Consider a *functional resume* instead of a *chronological* one.

Look up "functional resume" on the Internet. You will find tutorials everywhere for how to write one. And everyone needs one—from Boomers all the way to Millennials. Boomers are trying to highlight their experience and postpone their age being part of the hiring equation. Millennials are trying to pull together how their skills, schooling, volunteer work, and internship experiences add up to explain why they're capable of doing the job and contributing.

Even Gen X can benefit from a functional resume. But unlike Boomers, your generation doesn't need to hide your age on your resumes. It's already a non-issue—in fact, it's a plus. Employers list "10-15 years of experience" for a reason. You're in their "sweet spot." They don't have to train you, as they would a Millennial, but they also don't have to pay you as much as a Boomer who has more experience and whose health insurance will cost the company twice what yours will. If you have a mixture of job experiences, though, and you want to highlight specific ones that make you perfect for the job you're going for, then use a functional resume. It allows you to highlight what's important for the HR recruiter or hiring manager to consider about you.

Word of Warning about Functional Resumes: Some HR recruiters still view functional resumes as a warning sign:

- "The applicant must be trying to hide something, maybe an employment gap."
- "How recent is this experience? Is the applicant trying to hide the fact that they haven't done this in 10 years?"

If you fall in the "sweet spot" for the job you're applying for, by all means use a *chronological resume.* They'll see right away that there's nothing they need to be concerned with.

For those of you who don't fall into the "sweet spot," but you know you are qualified and really want a shot at that job, take a shot at it anyway with your *functional resume*—but use a cover letter. Emphasize there how you've done exactly what they're looking for in the job posting and how your experience makes you perfect for the position.

Tip 6: Write a cover letter.

- **Some will read it; some won't. Write one anyway.** For the companies that do read them, a cover letter can tip the scales in your favor toward getting your resume seen.

- **Use a T-table** to emphasize how great a fit you are for the preferred qualifications in the posting. This is what makes the cover letter work for you.

The T-table makes the case that your resume is worth reading and that you are worth considering. It connects specific requirements with proof

Chapter 7 — Resumes

that you are *very* qualified to meet them and, thereby, perform that job extremely well. Here are a couple of examples.

Requirement	My Qualifications
• 3-5 years experience teaching technical classes	• I taught software classes to IT professionals and project managers, as well as engineers for 5 years.
• Expertise in OSHA regulations	• As the Safety Engineer at a manufacturing firm, I kept our facility in compliance without a single OSHA citation in 4 years.

Tip 7: Tailor each resume for each submission. Use *exact* wording.

There's no such thing as a "one size fits all" resume any more. Tailor each one to each position you're applying for, as appropriate.

Use *exact* wording to match the job posting description. Here's the logic. The HR recruiters are probably experts in HR, but not experts in your field. Without wording matches, the recruiter may not be able to tell if your resume actually matches the job you're applying for.

Wordle (http://www.wordle.net/): Wordle will scan a job description and tell you the frequency of words and phrases in it. That can help you discern the employers' biggest emphasis for this position. Use those words in your resume. Don't overdo it, but repeat those exact phrases, as appropriate.

Wordle Word Cloud

1. Cut and paste job description into Wordle
2. Create Word Cloud
3. Create exact word match in your resume to prominent keywords in the Word Cloud

True story with a great outcome: A few years ago, I was asked by a hiring manager to submit an application for a job opening in her new Learning and Development Department. The HR recruiter called (in what seems like ancient history, recruiters actually had the time to contact applicants) and said she could not forward my resume to the manager because I was "not qualified" for the job. Not only was that distressing news, but it also directly contradicted what the hiring manager had said. The manager had said I looked so qualified that I was almost *overqualified*. Clearly there was a huge disconnect between the hiring manager's reading of my resume and the HR recruiter's.

To make a long story short, my manager-to-be and I got expert help from another HR recruiter. She revised my resume using *exact wording* wherever possible. I resubmitted it to HR. The recruiter saw the fit, passed the resume on to the manager, and I was hired.

In this job market, recruiters are receiving hundreds if not thousands of resumes for each available position. In larger companies, computer software will scan your resume for keyword matches before a recruiter will ever see it. By tailoring your resume based on the exact words used in the job description, you are increasing your chances of getting to the next step of the process.

Making the case and making the connection for the HR recruiter is *your* job.

If you know you're a good fit for a position, consider revising the wording in your resume so it's also obvious to an HR recruiter that you would be perfect for the job.

Chapter 8 — Interview Tips for Introverts

Here are my top seven potential interview challenges with recommended tips for introverted job seekers. I've field-tested these for three years in my *pro bono* work at a local job seekers' networking group. I'd like to thank all of my introverted clients who continue to validate and contribute solidly to the value of this list.

Top 7 Potential Challenges for Introverts during the Interview and What to Do About Them

Challenge 1: I hate the "deer in the headlights" experience. How do I avoid that?

> **Prepare, prepare, prepare.** The more prepared you are, the fewer "deer in the headlights" experiences you'll have.
>
> - **Prepare answers for "Behavioral Questions."** Google "64 Toughest Interview Questions." All over the Internet, you can find helpful suggestions for how to handle difficult questions during job interviews.
>
>   I know 64 seems overwhelming. Take, say, five a day. That's doable. Just go ahead and get started on it. They really are helpful and having well-prepared answers can mean the difference between going no further and getting a second interview.
>
> - **Research the company on the Internet.** If they're facing a potential merger, bring that up. It shows you did due diligence and that you're informed. If they had a great third quarter profit report, mention that. If you see news that spells real trouble, it could save you the hassle of applying to a situation you'd later regret getting into.

- **Research the HR rep and hiring manager on LinkedIn.** You can at least look at part of their information, even if you are not linked. Also, see if they're linked to anyone that you are already linked to. You can even search the company name for everyone you're linked to—first, second, or third level—who works there (and is in LinkedIn).

If you join networking groups and offer to help others, chances are you can find someone in your network who's willing to reach out for you. Just this morning, I forwarded a resume for a job-seeking colleague who had applied to a division that another colleague leads at a large software company. He had already applied to the job, but this action greatly increases the chance that he will "get eyes on" his resume. Remember, it's not that you're being rejected so much as you're not even being seen in many cases. The incoming applications stack is just too high in most areas to guarantee that a pair of eyes will come anywhere near your resume.

Challenge 2: What do I do when I need time to think before replying?

Introverts need more time to mull before answering than extraverts. That's just the way it is. Here are some tips that can help.

When you're prepared: If you've already thought about and prepared an answer, you can reply just as quickly as extraverts because your mulling work is already done. (This is just another benefit to preparing ahead!)

Techniques that work for introverts: That said, there are still going to be times when you need a moment to think. Introverts have shared with me several techniques they use that are effective for them:

- If you are not answering because you are mulling, then just say that—out loud. "Interesting question—I could use a moment to think about that."
- Some use the technique of repeating the question and asking, "Did I get that right?" It buys you time to think. Sometimes,

- it buys you just enough.
- One introverted client replied, "No, I've never had anyone interrupt me when I was mulling an answer in an interview." I said, "That's fascinating. Could you tell us what you do that helps you manage that so well?" She mulled for a moment and replied, "I tend to tilt my head up and to the side and say, "hmm." Everyone laughed, but seriously, that's brilliant. I'm no cultural diversity expert, but at least in the US, that's a pretty universally accepted signal for "I'm thinking about it."

Remember to give them the external clues they need: Finally, remember an important difference between you and extraverts. An extravert's sense of time is *so very* different from yours that they need to know "what you're doing" when you're silent. As ludicrous as this can seem at times to introverts, the extravert's process is something like, "What are they doing? Why aren't they answering? Oh, they must need me to rephrase the question." Seriously trying to be helpful, they start to speak again, interrupting your thought process. It's not helpful. Forgive them. They genuinely think they're helping when they do that. Perhaps I should say *"we" genuinely think we're helping.*

Challenge 3: What do I do when there's complete silence?

First of all, consider that the interviewer may be an introvert and, like you, may just be mulling and composing their thoughts. You know all about that, so let them.

After a respectful period of silence, you could help them out by asking, "Does that answer your question?" Or, perhaps, "Would you like another example of . . . ."

Challenge 4: Chitchat is hard for me when I don't know someone.

Yes, depending on your preferences, chitchat might be less comfortable for you than it is for some. Realize that small talk is not a bad thing. It can establish rapport and help the interviewer, who may be nervous as well, ease into a dialog with you. So participate.

I wouldn't *start* the chitchat if they don't. But if they do, then respond in kind. That kind of response to their lead could make them feel more comfortable with you.

When you can, bring the discussion back to the job. Either ask them a question or offer other examples of problems you've solved in other jobs that seem relevant to what they would be hiring you for. Remember that employers don't really want to "hire people." What they really want is to "solve problems." Use any chance you get to provide further evidence that you can handle what they need taken care of.

Challenge 5: What do I do when the interviewer is inexperienced?

Employee and management training has been done less and less in the past 10 years. You cannot assume the interviewer is experienced unless they are the actual HR recruiter. That said, you do need to tread carefully so as not to offend.

For example, an inexperienced interviewer may appear to fumble somewhat: they may have unusually long pauses, meander instead of using a more logical progression, struggle to find the "right question," or may not be comfortable enough to make eye contact. Be gentle, kind interviewee. If you try to "take over" the interview, that could come across as rude or as controlling.

There are multiple potential reasons for unskillful interviewing behavior:

- **Consider that the interviewer may be an introvert:** Seriously, they could just be an introvert mulling over their notes to see what to ask you next. Give them some silence. Don't immediately assume silence is a bad thing.

- **The interviewer may have received little or no training, even if they are a hiring manager:** Don't assume the interviewer has had training in conducting effective interviews. In the past ten years, companies have greatly reduced the amount of employee and management training they offer.

The interviewer may not be trained in interviewing techniques and may be just as nervous as you are.

- **Consider that they may just be new at this:** Perhaps the interviewer has had training but hasn't had the chance to put these skills to work. Do your best to put *them* at ease. In some cases, the interview may be just as challenging for them as for you. Give them silence if they seem to need it.

If the silence drags on: Gently bring the topic back to your accomplishments. Remember, this is your time to show that you're the right person for the job, so you deserve the chance to put in your two cents. You might also use the opportunity to ask a question about the company: "About the company, I was just wondering..." or "About the company, I'd appreciate your insights on..." Asking thoughtful, genuinely curious questions is rarely a bad thing.

You can also guide a struggling interviewer by offering examples of difficult situations you were able to resolve in a productive way. Have your PAR stories ready in case the interviewer seems to need help in getting good information out of you.[1] These are stories that let you show how you handled a situation and solved problems to achieve a desired result. Employers need people who can solve problems and achieve results. It helps you highlight the value you bring to the table.

Challenge 6: What do I say when they ask, "What have you been doing since you were laid off?"

Keep a list of what you accomplish during the job transition. Make a list of things you can say you were doing rather than just saying, "Looking for a job is a full-time job." Anyone who's been out of work in a recession knows how true that statement is, but you still need to be able to point out productive things you've accomplished.

---

1   PARs are stories in the form of Problem ⇒ Action ⇒ Result. You state the problem you faced at work, the actions you took to address the problem, and the results of your actions. Have multiple PARs ready for interviews.

One friend, for example, was taking care of aging parents for a few months during a transition period. Another spent a year renovating a house in the neighborhood so that they could turn it from a rental into a home for a new family. There are all sorts of honorable activities that could keep you out of the job market. Don't be ashamed of having been out of work. Just be prepared with things you can say you've been doing.

Making a list may sound silly, but you have no idea until you've been there how fast the week will go, how busy you'll feel, and how clueless you can be on Friday as to what you actually accomplished that week.

As a last benefit, it's a way to show all those family members who think you can run errands for them "because you don't have to work" that you *are* doing something and that you are not at their beck and call for errands all the time. You *do* actually "have a job." Your job is to find a job, a good job, one that is worthy of your talents and skills.

Volunteer for a non-profit or do *pro bono* work in your field:

- First, it shows a civic-mindedness and that can't be bad.
- Second, non-profits are hurting in this economy. They need all sorts of things done that they don't have funding for. I know an IT guy who did a special IT project for a non-profit; that *pro bono* work *in his field* showed up in LinkedIn as contract work, i.e., not sitting at home eating *bonbons*.
- Third, you never know whom you will meet there. You never know where that next contact is coming from; it may lead you to a job opening perfect for you, or to getting eyes on your resume, or to getting an important interview.
- Finally, it's impossible to feel helpless or bad about yourself when you're reaching out to do something helpful for someone else. (I learned that from the self-empowerment guru Tony Robbins.)

It's just win/win all the way around to do volunteer work or *pro bono* work, so go out there and support a cause you believe in and will feel good about contributing to.

Challenge 7: It's really hard for me to "sing my own praises." It feels like I'm bragging.

>**Take a deep breath.** You can do this. Sometimes people with clearly introverted preferences have a hard time praising themselves. Practice with a friend until you can say positive things about yourself with ease.
>
>**Make a list of your positive achievements** that would be relevant to a position you'd be applying for.
>
>**You're *not bragging;* you're *sharing information*** that communicates your ability to do good work for their company. You're just sharing data points. And that's okay. It helps the recruiter make the right decision about hiring you, and you deserve the best representation possible in that interview. It's really *not bragging*.

Chapter 9—Interview Tips for Extraverts

Here are my top eight potential interview challenges for extraverted job seekers. I've field-tested these for three years in my *pro bono* work at a local job seekers' networking group. As a flaming extravert by preference myself, I can say that I've actually *lived* these—both the pitfalls *and* the tips.

My workshops on interviewing tend to attract more introverts than extraverts. Introverts are more likely to perceive their preference as a potential handicap in an interview than extraverts. But there are natural pitfalls for extraverts, too. Extraverts are just more likely to think they don't have any.

Especially when being interviewed by someone with a more introverted preference, an extravert can offend or just plain miss the mark and end up perplexed about what went wrong. Here are eight common holes that extraverts tend to fall into and tips on what to do about them.

Top 8 Potential Challenges for Extraverts during the Interview and What to Do About Them

Challenge 1: It just seems to come right out of my mouth; then I regret it.

>**Extraverts tend to "think out loud."** This is *not* a metaphor. Extraverts literally talk their way through their own thought process to arrive at what they actually think. Because it's natural for them, they are likely unconscious of it, so they don't notice when it's not helpful and when they should reel it in. Consider the potential negative impact of that behavior in an interview.
>
>First, note your natural tendencies and *get conscious* so that you can choose how to respond instead of being guided unconscious-

ly by your natural patterns. By preparing before the interview, you get a lot of your natural "thinking out loud" done ahead of time. Now when you speak in the interview, more "editing" has been done and you can speak more confidently and take less time to say what you need to say.

When extraverts are nervous, they tend to do what they do naturally–only *louder* and *more of it.* That means "running off at the mouth" out of sheer nervousness. Be conscious of this tendency and don't let it draw you into talking more and louder.

To prevent your natural tendency to "just keep talking," when you become nervous, first, pay attention to what it feels like in your body when you feel compelled to keep talking. Once you become aware of your own internal feelings, you can choose to alter your behavior. The fix can be as simple as telling yourself to "just stop talking" when you feel the nervousness begin to set in. I can't tell you how many extraverts in my workshop have shared some version of

> **"I heard myself when I was doing it.
> I just couldn't stop.
> I listened to myself talk my way
> right out of landing that job."**

This is a classic sand trap for extraverts; don't fall into it.

Challenge 2: Why should I practice? I'm going to "wing it" anyway when I get in there.

>**Avoid the "winging it on a prayer and a promise" technique as much as possible.** Prepare and practice beforehand. Even if you tend to be good off the cuff, you can still benefit from preparation. I am definitely the pot calling the kettle black here. I *know* my own tendency to think "I'm going to wing it anyway." Trust me. Preparation and practice will make your "off the cuff" even better.
>
> - Prepare answers for "Behavioral Questions." Google "64

Toughest Interview Questions."
- Research the company on the Internet. Be ready to show that you're informed on important issues facing the company and important achievements they may have recently made.
- Research the HR representative and the hiring manager on LinkedIn. Do not underestimate the value of research and of LinkedIn in particular.

Challenge 3: What do I do about silences?

Be patient. Extraverts are naturally impatient about silences. Their sense of internal timing is so different from introverts that a normal silence to the introvert can seem like an eternity to an extravert. As a result, extraverts tend to talk nervously to fill the silence. This can have dire consequences.

Be aware of what it feels like inside you when you just *have to talk now.* Be conscious of your natural patterns and how the feeling "oh, I've got to talk now, I can't stand this silence anymore" arises in *your body.* It does have a visceral component. Develop a self-awareness of how this feels so that you can recognize it and consciously choose to correct it. Even when you feel that you absolutely have to talk, choose instead to remain still and not jump in—preventing yourself from over-talking and potentially offending the interviewer.

Let silences be. The interviewer may simply be pausing to consider which question to ask next. Or the interviewer may simply be an introvert who is pausing naturally to gather their thoughts before asking the next question.

Silence is not a bad thing, though it may seem like an eternity to an extravert. If you speak up just to fill it, you may be interrupting the interviewer's thought process and you may be talking your way right out of that job.

One thing you can do, if the silence really goes on and on, is ask, "Does that answer your question?" Then wait patiently for an answer.

Challenge 4: Why do others tend to take more time to respond? Why is their pace so much slower than mine?

Pace yourself in tune with the interviewer. The point is to connect with the other person so that you can develop rapport. Slowing down can help that tremendously. Extraverts tend to speak more quickly than introverts naturally. Stay in tune with the interviewer. If they speak more slowly than you do, then slow down as you reply.

Introverts need more time to respond because they do more internal processing naturally. Remember, for introverts, it's all happening on the inside. Your "thinking out loud" style is naturally faster because you don't tend to edit first.

No one is right or wrong. It's just a natural difference that you need to be aware of and, if necessary, pace yourself to be more in tune with the other person.

Challenge 5: Sometimes I seem to talk over or interrupt the other person.

Let the interviewer finish their thought entirely before you open your mouth to respond. Just as importantly, realize that you may be likely to stop listening altogether because you already know what you want to say and are only focusing on your answer. Consider the potential impact on the other person. They can already tell by the look on your face that you're not really listening anymore. They know you're just waiting for a chance to jump in and respond.

Sometimes extraverts even overlap the interviewer out of enthusiasm. Unfortunately, it can be misperceived as rude. So get conscious, reel in that natural tendency to speak before the other person has finished.

Challenge 6: I'm expressive, so it's obvious when I already know what I want to say.

> **Do not open your mouth and set your face, like you're about to dive into the answer any second.** Again, you can be misperceived as no longer listening to the speaker, but fully focused on your own answer. It might also seem like you are not serious enough about the topic to give your answer some real thought before blurting it out.
>
> Thanks to my experience with psychological type, *I* know you may be doing this because you're fully engaged or because you're an extravert and you naturally "think out loud." But it can be misinterpreted as impatient or inconsiderate by an introverted interviewer or even, at times, by an extraverted one. Again, there's no right or wrong—just a difference that can lead to misinterpretation and loss of rapport.

Challenge 7: What do I do when the interviewer is inexperienced and doesn't let me talk or get to why I'm perfect for the job?

> **Do not assume that your interviewer is experienced at interviewing** or has been given any training in interviewing. This can be a huge assumption on your part.
>
> Put an unskilled interviewer at ease. Overpowering an unskilled interviewer is not likely to be successful. Instead, try to increase their comfort level with you.
>
> The downside for you is that you may not get to "show your stuff" before the interview is over. Don't let an inexperienced interviewer prevent you from putting your best foot forward.
>
> If there's silence, don't assume you should try to fill it. Especially if the interviewer is an introvert, the silence could be a natural and normal thing. If the silences seem to be eating up your interview opportunity, you can simply bring the topic back to your accomplishments. Help the interviewer see the connection between what you bring to the table and what the position requires.

Show that you have the experience and skills to solve the kinds of problems the job entails.

Do not assume the recruiter is an expert in your field. Especially if the initial interview is with the recruiter or an HR employee, do not assume that that person is an expert in *your field*. They're probably an expert in HR, but not in your specialty. You need, therefore, to make sure you draw the connection as directly as possible between what the job requires and what you are capable of doing and have proven in the past that you can do. *Using exact verbiage from the job description cannot be over emphasized.*

An HR rep once told me, "You do not seem to be qualified, so I can't pass on your resume." The hiring manager, who already knew me, had told me, in response to the *same* resume, "You look qualified for *my* position, based on this experience."

The difference? The hiring manager was a specialist in my field. She could tell what a good fit I was. The HR rep could not. The fix? I was helped to revise the resume to use as much exact verbiage from the job description as possible. It worked. The HR recruiter could then see that I actually was qualified. My resume got through and I got the job–my dream job, as a matter of fact.

Challenge 8: What do I say when they ask, "What have you been doing since you've been out of work?"

Volunteer or do *pro bono* work in your field:

- It shows a civic-mindedness and that can't be bad.
- Non-profits are hurting in this economy. They need all sorts of things done that they don't have funding for. I know an IT guy who did a special IT project for a non-profit. The project that he did for them was reported in LinkedIn as contract work, i.e., not sitting at home eating bonbons. Don't assume that volunteering means licking envelopes. You can find opportunities even to do work in your field at some non-profits. Just find one you'll feel good about contributing to and go help out.

- You never know whom you will meet there. You never know where that next contact is coming from. You'll probably even meet some other people you enjoy and who can add value to your growing network.
- Finally, it's impossible to feel helpless or bad about yourself when you're reaching out to do something helpful for someone else. (I learned that from Tony Robbins, the self-help guru, when he was interviewed by Oprah.)

It's just win/win all the way around to do volunteer or *pro bono* work, so go out there and support a cause you believe in.

Keep a list of what you accomplish during the job transition. Make a list of things you can say you were doing rather than just saying, "Looking for a job is a full-time job." We know that that's true, but still, you need to be able to point to productive things you've done.

One friend was taking care of aging parents for a few months during a transition period. Another spent a year renovating a house in the neighborhood so they could turn it from a rental into a home for a new family.

There are all sorts of honorable activities that could keep you out of the job market. Don't be ashamed of having been out of work. Just be prepared with things you can say you've been doing.

Making a list may sound silly, but you have no idea until you've been there how fast the week will go, how busy you'll feel, and how clueless you can be on Friday as to what you actually accomplished that week.

As a last benefit, a list is a way to show all those family members who think you can run errands for them "because you don't have to work" that you *are* doing something and that you are not at their beck and call for errands all the time. You *do* actually "have a job." Your *job* is to *find a job,* a good job, one that is worthy of your talents and skills. That, in and of itself, is a full-time job.

Chapter 10—Your 30-Second Elevator Speech

This is your moment. Make an impression, be remembered. Some networking groups go around the room and give everyone about 30 seconds to introduce themselves in what's called "an elevator speech," a speech the length of an average elevator ride. I want you to be prepared for this and represent yourself well when you do it.

What's the point of this?

Done well, the elevator speech is your best shot at connecting with someone who can help you get access to an opportunity and vice versa. The point is to make a positive, memorable impact in a very brief period of time. Don't ramble. Don't go into ancient history. Just make it count.

As important as it is to make a positive impression, it's equally important to go with the attitude "How can I help someone here?" When you listen to their elevator speeches, you may realize you can help them get access inside a company or learn about an opportunity that you saw but that they may have missed. Be a giver—not a taker—and make a good impression. Those two objectives will take you far at networking events like these.

Your Basic Format

1. State your name.
2. State the job title or contract opportunity you want them to associate with you.
3. Give an interesting, memorable fact.
4. State your target companies or industries.
5. Restate your name; spell it if they're likely to get it wrong.
6. End with "I'm in LinkedIn."

Let's Break It Down

1. **State your name.** "Hi, I'm… " or "Good Morning, I'm… " Just state your name, short and sweet. Say it clearly; make sure it doesn't run together. For example, "Carol Linden" runs together. I've been known to say, "Good morning, I'm Carol, Carol Linden." Someone once responded, "Is that like 'Bond, James Bond'?" I laughed and then said, "No, but if I don't say it this way, 10 minutes from now you're going to call me either 'Linda' or 'Carolyn'." People are embarrassed to get your name wrong, so try to help them get it right the first time.

2. **State the job title you want them to associate with you.** Let's be clear: this is *not* a trip down memory lane. Do not look backward when you state your job title. Look *forward*. This is about your future. This is the kind of job you *want* to be associated with. You want to leave such an impression that everyone thinks of *you first* when they hear about an opportunity for which you'd be the perfect fit.

   I can't tell you how many elevator speeches I've heard that started with the past, and then the speaker moved on to say they didn't want to do that anymore. By that point, all of their time was up, and the message they left me with was so muddled that I had no idea what to help them with. This is *your moment* to connect yourself with the opportunity you really, really want. Look to the future and be clear about your direction, so everyone else can be clear about how to help.

3. **Give an interesting, memorable fact.** Give them a one-line, memorable fact that will make you stand out from everyone else in the room. The kind of fact depends on the kind of job or industry you're targeting. I've heard all sorts of wonderful, memorable facts:
   - "I'm a CPA who does not do taxes. Instead I… "
   - "I managed projects with budgets of 18 million dollars.
   - "I love helping clients find their dream jobs."
   - "I can help 18-year-olds target what they should focus on in college and potentially save their parents thousands of dollars

in courses or a major that was never right for that student."

4. **State your target companies or industries.** This is how you help people help you. Targeting specific companies helps others know immediately if there's a way they can help "get eyes on" your resume. They'll think of colleagues they know in that industry you should talk to. It's okay if you show up next week with different targets. Just remember to be specific, so others will know how to help.

5. **Restate your name; spell it if they're likely to get it wrong.** People are embarrassed to ask your name, especially if you've already stated it once. Help them out. Repeat your name at the end to make it easier for them. If you have a tricky name, spell it. Help them find you in LinkedIn that way. I tend to say "Carol Linden—L-I-N-D-E-N like the tree." I say that because no one has spelled my family's name right since Lyndon B. Johnson was president.

6. **End with "And I'm in LinkedIn."** LinkedIn membership is becoming the status quo for business professionals. At some point, this will be assumed and won't need to be said. But for now, go ahead and remind them you're on LinkedIn, so they can know how to connect with you even if they didn't get your business card at the event.

True story of a blah elevator speech turned into a powerful one

A job-seeking colleague of mine got the courage to go to a local networking group called TAFU (To Avoid Future Unemployment). He was required to stand and give a 30-second elevator speech to the room.

His first time attending the group, he had his speech ready:

> *Hello, I am Roy Long and I was a business analyst at <a local telecom>. I'm targeting financial analyst positions at Company X and Company Y. Again, I'm Roy Long and I'm in LinkedIn.*

Afterward, another job seeker came up to him and said, "That is the most boring elevator speech I have ever heard."

Now, I don't know how you would have reacted to a criticism like that, your first time out in a new venue, but I, personally, would have gotten my feelings hurt. Roy did something much more productive than that. He decided he was receiving useful information and acted on it.

The next time he went to a TAFU meeting, he stood and said,

> *Hello, I'm Roy Long and I'm a business analyst. While at <a local telecom>, I served on a team that saved the company 6.24 million dollars in export taxes. I'm targeting business analyst positions at Company X and Company Y. Again, I'm Roy Long, and I'm in LinkedIn.*

The key to being remembered and getting people's attention is to provide a memorable fact that sets you apart. Your fact may be measurable in terms of dollar amounts or number of accounts served. Or it may be more qualitative, like a funny fact about what you do or how you do it differently. Roy was never again told that his pitch was "boring." I first heard it three years ago, and I've never forgotten how much money he saved a telecom company.

Your memorable fact doesn't have to mention money, as not everyone's job lends itself to that. You just need one detail that sets you apart. Either wow them or make them smile. My personal fact is:

> *Hello, I'm Carol Linden and I help adults play well with others.*

No one forgets that. They may get my company name wrong, but they laugh at my "tag line" and always remember me for it.

Chapter 11—When You Don't Know What You Want to Do Next

What do I want to do when I grow up?

I can't tell you how many job seekers I've worked with who have said some version of *I don't want to continue what I've been doing for the past 20 years, but I have no idea what I want to do next.*

The tragedy is that some of those folks were still saying the same thing 12 months later, still unemployed. The unfortunate cause of their continued unemployment is that indecision.

> **If you want to hit the mark,
> you have to know what you're aiming at.**

Think of the resume as your marketing tool. How can you write marketing material for yourself if you're not exactly sure *what* you're marketing, or even what audience you're marketing to? The inconvenient truth is that if you don't want to continue in the same line of work you've been doing, you're going to have to take the time to explore and figure out what you really want.

> **Decide what you want to do *before*
> you write your resume and apply to jobs.**

I realize this sounds so obvious that it shouldn't need to be said. It must need to be said, though, because it's heart-breaking to witness the number of Boomers still unemployed a year later, and still not sure what they want to do. There's a reason for that. In fact, there are three common reasons for that.

The three top reasons job seekers give themselves for *not* taking the time to decide what they really want to do:

1. Self-exploration seems impractical when you want to be back out there earning money as quickly as possible.
2. Many job seekers put off a full-scale self-exploration because they just do not know where to start.
3. It can be tough work figuring out *what* you want to do and *how* to get yourself there. Too many unknowns can be daunting, even paralyzing. I don't say this to scare you. I say this so you'll know that you're not alone in these feelings.

The Money Issue

Let's tackle the looming pragmatic issue first: money. Many job seekers see the time it takes to explore what they really want as impractical. Getting a job seems practical; figuring out what they really want seems like a luxury they can't afford. And so they put it off. They keep applying for jobs with a resume that was designed for a job they don't want.

Delayed gratification: The problem is that unless you take the time to figure out what kind of job you really, really want, shaping a resume that helps land that job will be difficult if not impossible. Figuring out what you want to do may appear to be delaying your next paycheck, but it's actually a smarter investment of your time than continuing to apply for jobs you don't even want.

In psychology it's called *delayed gratification*. Stanford studies have shown a correlation between a child's ability to delay gratification and that child's success later in life. If you can delay the gratification of *making money now,* you'll get a chance to invest your time wisely and be more prosperous in the future—in the job you really want.

Consider a survival job while you look for the *right job*: To be fair, your resistance to the idea of delaying the paycheck is primarily about *survival.* Needing money to survive can invoke a panic reaction that interferes with rational thinking. You're experiencing Maslow's hierarchy of needs: when you're in survival mode, it's hard to think about higher level needs, like laying the groundwork for a better future job instead of grasping for an immediate paycheck. Take heart. You can lay the groundwork and also get paid in the interim. You can have both.

With a survival job to reduce the financial pressure, you can use your time off to work steadily on figuring out what you really want and how to get it. In fact, think of figuring this out as a part-time job. Approach it as you would another job—one that will prove to be richly rewarding in your future success and happiness. Please believe me when I say that *you are worth* the investment.

Where to Start and Resources That Can Help

There are tons of resources out there to help you, including books, websites, workshops, and various psychological instruments. Where I live, we are blessed with community colleges that offer wonderful workshops that target the unemployed, and most of them are offered at no cost to the unemployed or under-employed.

Consider making use of

- Workshops at your local community colleges
- Courses through adult education programs at universities
- An outplacement service, if your former employer offers it
- An experienced career counselor
- Psychological instruments such as the MBTI and the Gallup StrengthsFinder.

Self-Exploration through the MBTI and StrengthsFinder: I find the Myers-Briggs (MBTI) and the Gallup StrengthsFinder to be very helpful to my clients in their self-discovery process. The MBTI (Myers-Briggs Type Indicator) and the Gallup StrengthsFinder instruments measure very different things, but they complement each other powerfully and can provide valuable insights for your self-discovery process. If you have never taken the MBTI, please look for a practitioner in your area at www.aptinternational.org. You can also contact me through www.effectivewithpeople.com.

I recommend the following books for getting insight into what your talents and natural preferences are:

- ***What's Your Type of Career?** : Find Your Perfect Career by Using Your Personality Type*, 2nd Edition, by Donna Dunning, Nicholas Brealey America, September 2010.

    Psychological type is my field, so I love that Dunning shows how your natural preferences can be a great tool for discovering the kind of work that could be a great fit for you. Richard N. Bolles, author of the famous *What Color is Your Parachute*, writes, "This is the best written, most insightful, and most helpful book I have ever read about using 'type' in the workplace." Author William Bridges writes, "Donna Dunning offers new and helpful assistance to anyone who wants to base a career on who he or she really is." It is with great confidence that I recommend Donna's book to you.

- ***StrengthsFinder 2.0***, by Tom Rath, Gallup Press, February 2007.

    I have used the Gallup StrengthsFinder reports with my clients for over seven years. It not only confirms what you may already know about your own strengths, but also points out strengths so central to who you are that they might even be invisible to you. I highly recommend this as a tool of self-discovery. Buying the book provides you with access to taking the instrument online. You can also go straight to the Gallup website and take the instrument there: www.gallupstrengthscenter.com. Gallup will email you a report on your top five talents. (Note: a Strength = Talent + Knowledge + Skill + Practice.)

More Resources: For a list of additional books and websites that can help you in this self-discovery journey, see ***Recommended Resources***.

A True Story: Changing Careers through Development and Networking

I worked in technical documentation for 19 years, first as a technical writer, then as a leader of technical writing teams, and finally as a department manager. Over time, I came to be less interested in what we were writing *about* and more interested in *how* I could help people work better together. I wanted to move from technical writing into training and development. I wanted to coach managers and leaders on how to understand each other better and how to lead their teams to work more cohesively. I was very passionate about making the change. There was one big problem.

**I didn't have a clue how to get a job
in a field I had never worked in before.**

To top it off, my change of heart came when the dot-com bubble burst in 2000-2001 and made it seem all but impossible to create such a career transition for myself.

Once again, networking came to my rescue. (To be candid, I had no idea I was networking. I thought I was just having conversations.) I remembered a woman who'd been a great management trainer during my early years as a manager. She was someone I trusted, so I called her and asked to have a conversation. I told her about my desire to coach managers and teams on how to better understand each other by using psychological type. I had experience as a team leader and I had taken many workshops and even completed certifications in facilitation, team building, and Myers-Briggs. For years, I'd been investing in myself in order to create the proper skillset for this line of work. Bear in mind that I was only talking with her because I trusted her and valued her advice. I had no idea at the time that she was putting together a new department that would be a perfect fit for my new career. And she was thrilled to have someone with my experience in this new learning and development department.

Long story short, I was so passionate about helping teams learn to work better together that I discussed it with two vice presidents, and eventually gathered the courage to ask the CEO to create a new position for me. It worked. I got a job as a *cross-functional team coach*—a position neither the hiring manager nor the CEO had heard of before I proposed it. In other words, I created the opportunity for a job that was not listed and, frankly, would never have been listed.

Some of the best jobs you'll ever have a chance at getting may not have been listed anywhere yet. That's why networking is important. I landed my dream job with two important actions:

- Investing in my own development
- Having honest conversations with people before I even knew they'd be able or willing to help.

While I thought I was just confiding in people I trusted, it turns out that I was networking my way into creating my dream job. You might consider this same approach: have honest conversations with people about something you're passionate about long before there's a job in sight. You have no idea what you might create this way, and until you start having these conversations, you'll never get the chance to know.

Don't wait until the path from A to B is already paved before you take the first step. That could be a very long wait. In fact, it might not even happen because your focus, intentions, and actions are what actually *create* the path. So just jump in and talk to people. That's what networking is.

Chapter 12 — Working with Recruiters

Recruiters can be very helpful. Sometimes recruiters are HR personnel who work inside a company, but here I'm talking about external recruiters. Client companies pay them fees when they help fill a valuable position with a suitable candidate. If you intend to work with one, you should keep a few things in mind to help prevent wasting your time or theirs and to keep your expectations realistic.[1]

Things to keep in mind when working with a recruiter:

- **Understand the volume they're dealing with and don't take things personally.** The CEO of one local independent recruiting firm reported that on average, they had to look at *eighty* job candidates for every *one* they placed. Think about those numbers. They cannot possibly call everyone back. So don't take it personally when you don't hear back from them, especially if they don't have an opening that is a real fit for you.

- **Only pursue a position with a recruiter when you are a great fit and are well qualified for that position.** Recruiters make money when they place people. Period. They are in business and trying to make a living. They need a candidate who is as perfect a fit as possible. If you're not really a good fit for a job, you are pursuing a "long shot." Trying to place a candidate who is a "long shot" for a position does not help them stay in business, nor does it help you succeed in getting the job that is right for you.

- **Your skillset and experience need to be recent and relevant.** Their clients (employers) pay a premium fee for candidates who have recent experience and a relevant skillset in the appropriate industry. If you are that candidate (and be really honest with yourself about that for each position you're vying for), then you could have a very positive and productive experience with a re-

---

1   Sincere thanks to Cindy Smith Waite, President of Accentuate Staffing in Raleigh, NC for contributing her expertise on this topic.

cruiting firm.

- **Consider working with a recruiter who specializes in your area of expertise or industry.** You could form a professional relationship that could help you throughout your career. Recruiters, especially those in a specific field or industry, form relationships with highly skillful professionals in the hopes of doing business with them in the future. The norm is going to become having many jobs and multiple employers, not one long career in one large company. Forming a relationship with a reputable recruiter in your field could benefit you throughout your career.

When it's not so helpful to try to work with a recruiter:

- **When you don't know what you want to be when you grow up.** Working with a recruiter is not productive when you're uncertain about what you're really aiming for. In that case, you need a good career counselor, not a recruiter. I would start at the career office where you attended college or at the local community college in the area where you live.

- **When you're not a great fit for the position.** Long shots do not help you get a job through a recruiter and only serve to annoy their clients, the employers. Do both of you a favor: only attempt to go for a position through a recruiter when you really are qualified and your experience is both *recent* and *relevant*.

- **When you present yourself as a "jack of all trades."** Seriously, there are *very few* listings for "jack of all trades." Recruiters need you to be specific and be willing to focus on a certain skillset and have the experience to back up your claim to be a "good fit" for a certain position.

When using a recruiter is most helpful:

When you are focused, even if applying for different types of jobs. Even if you are open to taking more than one kind of job, you have to present yourself in a coherent and focused way *for* *each one.* You need different resumes for different kinds of positions. Each one focuses on your skills and experiences for that specific position.

Each resume should duplicate the *exact wording* found in each job description, so you'll need a different resume for each specific job you're applying for. Remember that HR recruiters are not specialists in your field. They are specialists in their field: HR recruiting. They are looking for *exact wording matches* to see that you are indeed a good placement for a job in a field outside of their expertise.

Best tips for working with a recruiter:

- Show up with the right attitude. What's the right attitude? Not down and out, yet not entitled either. Be positive. Be professional.

- Keep yourself foremost in their minds in a positive way. You want to remind them that you exist so they'll think of *you* when they see another potential fit for your qualifications and experience.

    Here are some examples of messages that keep you in the front of their mind in a positive way.

    - "Hi, just wanted you to know that I'm still interested in that project manager position that we were pursuing at Company X. Give me a call if I can help you: (999) 999-9999. No need to call me back. Have a great week, John."

    Note: your phone number is in the message to make it easy for them to contact you, but you are not asking for or demanding a call back.

    - "Hi, just wanted you to know that I'm still in the job market and very interested in other project management positions you see me as a potential fit for. Give me a call if I can help you: (999) 999-9999. No need to call me back. Have a great week, John."

Note: again, your phone number is in the message to make it easy for them to contact you, but you are not asking for or demanding a call back.

Note what these messages do *not* do. They do not

- Add to the recruiter's endless to-do list for that day.

- Project frustrations or other negative emotions onto the recruiter. (Who's going to want to remember you if every message carries a negative emotion?)

- Lay a guilt trip on the recruiter. (Who needs *more guilt* in their lives? Most people have a parent, spouse, or child for that.)

- **Do not annoy them.** Related to the preceding point, leaving a message that tries to lay a guilt trip on them is not helpful. Now they *remember you*, but not in a way that is productive for you. Do not leave a message that tries to make them feel guilty for not getting back in touch with you or that shows your annoyance in any way.

Here are some **concrete examples of messages *not* to leave** on their voice mail or send in an email:

- "This is John. I haven't heard back from you and just wondered how it was going with that position you were helping me pursue at Company X. Please call me as soon as you can."

- "This is John. This is the third message I've left and I really need to hear back from you. Please call me about that position…"

Note that these messages create an extra to-do item for the recruiter that day, as well as leave a negative emotion associated with you. To work effectively with recruiters, try to leave positive messages that convey your willingness to work with them.

Chapter 13 — Hindsight is 20/20

11 Things Job Seekers Wish They'd Done Differently

We all know that hindsight is 20/20. That said, I'd love for someone to learn from my mistakes and those of others who have tread this path before you. I surveyed members of a large jobseekers' networking group in North Carolina where I've volunteered for 4 years. I hope that offering you this collective wisdom helps make your job transition shorter, smoother, and less arduous. *Namaste.*

1. **Build a network, expand your network, and nurture your network when you're unemployed** *as well as when you are employed.*
2. **Pay it forward.**
3. **Assess your financial situation more quickly.**
4. **Get over the "why me?" syndrome sooner, grieve your losses, and move on.**
5. **Develop a plan of action and set a structure for your days.**
6. **Get an accountability partner sooner instead of later.**
7. **Retool yourself for a 21st century search and keep learning.**
8. **Stay active professionally.**
9. **Get over the fear of rejection.**
10. **Know that getting work is easier than getting a job.**
11. **Volunteer!**

11 Things to Do Sooner Instead of Later

1. **Build a network, expand your network, and nurture your network when unemployed** *as well as employed.* For the first six months, I made calls, set appointments, and met *only* with people who were already in my own professional network. Not that that's a bad thing. I had a decent-sized network because I'd been so active in professional organizations in my chosen field. That said, I wish I'd realized sooner that I needed to expand my network and include other people. I wish I'd gotten engaged in networking groups in the area right away.

I imagine I could have made progress sooner if I'd done that.

Other networkers have said they realized after an earlier layoff that they should have continued networking. Instead, they let their connections grow cold. Consequently, when the next layoff came, they had to try to warm up their old network or re-build a new network from scratch.

I have a colleague who managed to get rehired within one year after each of three layoffs. How? One job came from someone she hadn't seen in eight years. Another job, from someone she hadn't seen in 10 years. But she'd kept up with everyone, emailing them information and links she thought might interest them. She'd continued nurturing her network, so it was there for her when she needed it. She didn't have to start over each time. Having a vital network is necessary for the new marketplace, where we're all going to be looking for work more often than in the past.

2. **Pay it forward.** At first, the sense of "I have to have a job *right away*" overrides everything. That's normal. But understand sooner instead of later that you need to walk into every networking event with the attitude, "How can I help someone here?" It's called "paying it forward." And it works. At some point, we're all going to need the kindness of strangers to make a connection for us. Start paying it forward right away. Your time will come. It's karma, baby, karma in *your* favor.

3. **Assess your financial situation more quickly.** Nearly everyone says, "I would have cut expenses more quickly if I had realized how long this might last and how hard it might be to get reemployed."

I wish for everyone reading this that your job transition lasts only a few weeks—or two to three months max—and that you don't experience financial stress or tap into savings or your 401K. That said, this is a moment in history. Many job seekers are experiencing a marathon instead of a sprint, especially Baby Boomers and Millennials. Even Gen X is taking longer to land a job than before. Savings and 401K plans alike are being depleted.

Whether your job transition is a sprint or a marathon, cutting expenses sooner instead of later will bear good fruit for you. If you're on a marathon, it will make your severance pay and unemployment benefits last longer. If you're on a sprint, cutting expenses means you'll be ahead of the game when you do land.

4. **Get over the "why me?" syndrome sooner, grieve your losses and move on.** Whether you're a Boomer who's taking much longer than you'd like to get rehired, a Gen Xer who's out longer than seems reasonable, or a Millennial who's struggling even to get into a job, you can easily fall prey to the "why me?" syndrome. Try to remember that *it's not about you*. We're all still recovering from the worst recession since the Great Depression. The issue we're facing is historical, not personal—even though the impact is profoundly personal. Remind yourself of that and don't let it damage your self-esteem.

Some of you may have had more painful transition experiences than others. If so, your losses are very real. It's not just losing a regular paycheck and immediate financial security. You also lose meaningful friendships with coworkers and the sense of belonging you felt with them—sometimes literally overnight. You may feel that you've been "voted off the island" and your future is suddenly insecure and uncertain.

There truly are things to grieve. Go ahead, feel the pain, and grieve. It's not easy, and you will go into denial and try to avoid the grief work. But take it from someone who's been there: do it sooner instead of later. Grief unexpressed will cause far more pain in your life than the pain you'll feel if you actually open up, let yourself feel it, and let it go. There are great books and even grief groups to help you get through this.

Don't be ashamed or afraid to explore this. Grieving does not make you weak. In fact, it takes a lot of courage to face grief instead of suppress it. As a result, you'll be less afraid, you'll have more energy, and you'll free yourself up to be your best self when you show up to an interview.

5. **Develop a plan of action and set a structure for your days.** The days will fly by. You'll get to Friday, will have felt busy all week, and

have no idea what you have to show for it. Structure your days. Get up, get dressed, put your game face on. Don't give in to the temptation to sit at your computer and submit online applications all day. Applications that aren't backed up by additional work, such as networking, have very little chance of succeeding in this economic environment. Balance your time between searching online, sending in applications, working on your resumes, and networking.

6. **Get an accountability partner sooner instead of later.** Get a job seeker buddy or a good friend *who is capable of understanding what you're going through* to be your accountability partner. You'll set goals and get them done and report back to each other. It's a system that works. Note: this person is not your significant other. If you are out of work, your significant other is under stress too. A conversation between two stressed people concerned about money can be very unproductive. It is best to draft a fellow job seeker and be a good accountability partner in return.

7. **Retool yourself for a 21st century search and keep learning.** You need to be in LinkedIn. It's not optional; it's required now. You'll be able to find second level connections that will help you "get eyes on" your resume in your target companies. Get in there, link to others, and network your way into a company.

    One of the things employers say about the long-term unemployed is that they're afraid their skills are out of date. Show them that's not true. Look to your local community colleges, adult continuing education centers at major universities, online classes, and workshops offered by professional organizations for its members. You'll be amazed at what technical things you can learn online and even from YouTube, and all for free.

8. **Stay active professionally.** Remain involved in professional groups related to your past career or get active with professional groups for the career you hope to move into. This will give you an opportunity to find out about open positions before they get posted or to meet someone who can "get eyes on" your resume. Also, going to learning events and meetings shows that you are staying up to date in your field.

9. **Get over the fear of rejection** so that you can put yourself out there sooner and more often. You may get more *nos* than *yeses* when you first start out. We all have to learn to think like Thomas Edison. A *no* is not a defeat. It's one step closer to getting a *yes*, eventually. Hanging back will only prolong the unemployment period and make this all the more painful in the long run.

10. **Getting work is easier than getting a job.** Initially I was stuck in the paradigm that I knew: "get a job." The distinction between *a job* and *work* had never been drawn for me. Times were hard in 2009 and 2010 when I was first unemployed and job seeking; interviews were few and far between. In fact, the only interviews I landed during those early, dark days came from personal contacts I made at networking and professional training events. I met one recruiter and one new employee at companies I'd targeted. Getting only two interviews in 15 months was very discouraging. (Don't be unduly disheartened by this, as it isn't likely to happen to you. The jobs in my field were still disappearing at that point in time.)

    My experience changed dramatically, however, when I started inquiring about work opportunities instead of jobs. For example, when I looked into teaching contract courses for a psychological type consulting company, being adjunct faculty at a community college and a hired consultant at two other universities, I simply could not get no for an answer.

    I'm not talking about survival jobs here, although those do have their place. I'm talking about contract work, in your chosen field, drawing on your core strengths and expertise. If Ed Weems, adjunct faculty of entrepreneurial studies at NCSU and NCCU, had not taught me this principle, I wouldn't have reached out in this way to consulting companies and three universities. And I would have really missed out, not only on some decent, if sporadic, income, but also on some great experiences and connections to people I would greatly enjoy and who could vouch for the value I add. I also got a great opportunity to further develop my materials and gather even more client stories for future workshops.

11. **Volunteer!** I really stumbled into this, but what a great stumble! Get

out there and volunteer. Job seekers I've known have received incredible benefits from volunteer work, including ending up with a real job for that organization or a valuable connection to someone they met there.

You're probably thinking, "Looking for a job is a full-time job. When will I have time to volunteer?" And, frankly, you'd be right to think that. But you can't stare into a computer screen 40 hours a week—at least, it won't be very productive to spend your time that way. And you can't network 40 hours a week, either. Instead, you can find a few hours to contribute to the community, meet some new people, and get uplifted by helping others. It raises your spirits and your self-esteem, and there's no telling where that next connection will come from. Also, you need a good answer for, "What have you been doing since you've been out of work?" This way, you can say more than just "looking for a job."

Chapter 14—Especially for Millennials: How to Get into the Job Market

If you're a Millennial and wondering why you still don't have a "real job," not just a survival job, don't beat yourself up about it. This is the worst hiring market since the Great Depression. (And, *no*, I did not experience that one personally.)

True Story: How I Got a "Real Job"

I had a great deal of frustration trying to get into the job market myself back in the 80s. I was in an over-educated market and to top it off, I had a liberal arts degree (fashionable at the time). In my mother's words, "The only thing that Sewanee degree is good for is for you to sit on the veranda and think thoughty thoughts." Evidently, many employers thought so too. It was a real struggle for me to break into the professional job market—not unlike what's going on for Millennials now.

It took me three years to make my way from student work, through part-time survival work, through full-time survival work, and eventually to a real professional job. So take heart: it can be done, and it is being done, even in this market. It's just going to take effort and creativity, and it's going to take longer than your parents think it should. (It's not their fault. They probably grew up in a bull market when stock prices were rising and companies were hiring. For most of them, taking so long to get a job is new, especially if they had a more obviously employable major in college than I did.)

The Process

How did I break into the job market? It was a five-step process:

1. Informational interviews
2. Internship
3. Part-time survival jobs, building experience for my field

4. Full-time survival jobs, still building experience for my field
5. Networking inside a company

Informational interview: I did an informational interview with a senior editor at the Institute of Government at UNC-CH. She seemed like a potentially good source of information on how to break into writing and editing. She was kind enough to grant me the time to sit down and talk.

Note: Because it was an informational interview, I had made it very clear that I wasn't looking for a job, but was asking instead to learn from her expertise. That is important. *Never* ask for an informational interview and then start behaving like you're asking for a job. If they feel misled by your intentions, their trust in you will be damaged and they'll feel less willing to help you.

After looking at my resume, she told me she would want to see some printing experience on a resume before she would hire someone as an editor. (Editing, writing, I was open to any entrée into the field at the time.) I thanked her for her time and went about implementing what she suggested.

Internship: I took the editor at her word and began looking for an opportunity to learn how to set type. I found an internship at a local newspaper, so I learned to typeset there that summer. I didn't get paid, but it was a fair trade because I gained valuable experience. I didn't *want* to be a typesetter; I wanted a writing job, and typesetting proved to be the means to that end.

Part-time and full-time survival jobs: Thanks to the internship, I had the training and experience to get first a part-time and then a full-time job in typesetting. I had typesetting jobs at two local printing companies while I was trying to find my way into a writing job. As far as survival jobs go, typesetting paid decent money. Please note that there's nothing wrong with a typesetting job being your end goal. It can be interesting and creative work. It is also very detail-oriented work, and since I am naturally a big-picture person, it wasn't right for my skillset. I could do it, but the work itself exhausted me. So I used typesetting as a stepping stone to work I was better suited for. And what a great stepping stone it was. I'm glad I learned more about usable and visually attractive form,

Chapter 14—Especially for Millennials: How to Get into the Job Market

as "printing" on the Web now is just as important as printing on hard copy then.

Network inside a company: I did eventually make my way into a writing job at a software company. How? *Networking*. A friend worked there, ran into the technical writing department manager in the café, and simply said that he had a friend who wanted to make her way into a professional writing job. He asked the manager if she had any suggestions. She said she had an opening and to bring in the resume. He was able to *get eyes on* my resume, which gave me the opportunity to be considered for an interview. This domino effect in my favor happened all because someone inside the company spoke to a hiring manager for me. It's called *networking inside a company*. To be candid, only in hindsight did I realize how and why this was so effective. In the current job market, networking inside a company is standard practice and all but required.

The hiring manager saw that I had a liberal arts degree. She didn't need someone who could write software. She needed someone who could be a buffer between the programmer and the end user. She figured that with my degree, surely I had learned how to write. (So if you, too, have a *mere* liberal arts degree, take heart. There are employers open-minded enough to believe those degrees come with useful, employable people.) I even had publishing industry experience as a typesetter. I got the interview, she became convinced that I could do the work, and I got the job. While my experience and qualifications landed me the job, it was networking that gave me the opportunity to prove I deserved the job.

Taking Action: More than Just Submitting Applications Online

Instead of just submitting one application after another online, you're going to have to take additional, more creative steps. Consider these activities:

Ask for an informational interview with someone in a field you're considering. It's a time-honored way to have a conversation with someone without either party feeling pressure to make a decision. Prepare for that meeting. Know what you want to ask.

Consider questions like the following: How did you get into this field of work? What do you like most about your work? What's the culture like at your job? If you had it to do over again, would you do anything differently with regard to your field or your work? What can I do to prepare for a job in this field? Is there anyone else you think it would help me to speak with?

Ask for a mentoring conversation with someone who is working in a field you'd like to enter. Do this the right way. Make all the effort yourself. Offer to buy the person coffee or lunch, as the cost should be on the protégé. You'll be surprised at how willing people are to talk about how they entered their field and extend advice that might help you. Ask to connect with them in LinkedIn.

Attend meetup groups in your area. These aren't just recreational groups. You can find ones related to many different fields and types of work. Go to meetings, hear talks, find people who are already working in the field you want to work in. A side benefit for you is that the crowd at most meetups is younger, which means they work for companies that are willing to hire younger workers. Ask for their card; ask to connect with them in LinkedIn. You'll be amazed at how fast your second-level connections start accumulating when you start connecting with others in LinkedIn.

Connect with alumni groups and with alumni who are already working in the field. One of my Millennial colleagues recently got a chance at an interview through an older alumnus who was already working for a private company in her field. Reaching out to that older colleague led directly to the interview. Join alumni groups through your college and through LinkedIn. Participate in the online discussions. Connect with alumni working in the kind of industry you'd like to enter or who work for a company you're interested in. These used to be called "old boy networks," but of course they consist of both "boys and girls" now.

Find that internship. If it's a true internship, i.e., a chance to do work that expands your knowledge and experience and gets you a chance at a "real job," it's worth it. In recent times, it has become even harder to get a job without a proven track record in the kind of work you really want. Doing an internship may just be your ticket.

Chapter 14—Especially for Millennials: How to Get into the Job Market

Consider doing volunteer or *pro bono* work in your chosen field. Volunteer work isn't just about licking stamps and stuffing envelopes anymore. Non-profits are hurting right now for funding. They have fewer donations and volunteers in this economy because Baby Boomers have less disposable income and just aren't able to contribute, and Millennials are struggling to get into the market to get disposable income so that they can afford to contribute. There are many different types of work you could do for non-profits—professional work like Web design, fund raising, building applications, or managing special projects.

Consider a cause you really believe in and find out how you can be of service. As a side benefit, you never know who you'll run into there, or where that next open door will come from. At the very least, you'll get to contribute to a worthy cause and you'll probably meet some people you enjoy along the way.

Join professional associations in the field you want to enter and attend meetings and workshops. When I was a technical writer, I belonged to STC (Society for Technical Communications). When I wanted to move into training and developing and teaching people how to understand each other, several *years* before I was able to get a job in that field, I joined and attended meetings for APTi (Association for Psychological Type, International), ODNet (Organization Development Network), ATD (Association for Talent Development), and the board of a local quality council that focused on what was called "the soft side of quality," i.e., how to help people work together. If you don't know the names of such organizations in your chosen field, ask around. Meeting people in those organizations and learning with them can go a long way toward helping you enter a professional field and find a job you enjoy.

Get eyes on **your resume so that you can be seen.** When you think about how many rejections you're getting or, more likely, how many applications you're submitting online that are getting no answers at all, remember:

>**It's not that you're being rejected.
It's that you're not being seen.**

There are still so many applications for every open position that HR recruiters are overwhelmed with the workload. (HR departments were downsized, too.) Your two main goals should be to:

1. *get eyes on* your resume
2. get a chance at a job that hasn't even been listed yet.

Networking makes both of these possible.

Get yourself in LinkedIn. You need a presence in LinkedIn and a headshot that makes you look like an adult someone would have confidence in hiring. If you're a young Millennial, you may have only your education and interest groups to list there, but that's okay. If you do volunteer work, list it. If you belong to professional associations or work-related meetup groups, by all means, mention them. Anything you did in school that relates to the kind of work you want, make sure you record it in LinkedIn.

Network your way inside a company. Once you've found a specific job to apply for, network your way to a hiring manager or an HR recruiter inside that company. You can use LinkedIn to do this. To help get you started, watch LinkedIn tutorials on YouTube or take a LinkedIn class at a local community college.

And when you get there…

After you land a job—and you will, you really will—turn around and extend a hand to someone else who's looking for help to get into the job market. Build your network, ask for help, and be willing to give help for nothing in return. This is how to pay it forward and build a more connected world, one that is capable of helping you land your next job in the future. With all the fear and uncertainty this difficult market has created, this may just be the best thing that comes out of it—that we are more connected and more willing to help complete strangers and colleagues than we were in the past. We're going to need this kind of world. Let's build it together, one connection at a time.

Recommended Resources

Resources here include information about the following topics

- The Job Search Process
- Job Posting Sites
- Job Seeker Groups
- When You Don't Know What You Want to Do Next
- Introverts and Extraverts
- Psychological Resources
- Spiritual Resources

The Job Search Process

Levinson, Jay Conrad and David E. Perry. ***Guerrilla Marketing for Job Hunters 3.0***. New Jersey: John Wiley & Sons, Inc., 2011.

> Especially if you do not have access to classes or outplacement services, or even if you do, I highly recommend this book by Levinson and Perry. Use it to get up to speed quickly so that you don't waste weeks or months just submitting applications online.
>
> I would seriously recommend using this book in combination with Pierson's ***Team Up!*** Share your knowledge and work in a group to help encourage each other and promote accountability.

Pierson, Orville. ***Team Up!*** Massachusetts: Highly Effective Job Search, 2014.

> Especially if there are no job networking groups available to you, I highly recommended you gather a group around yourself and help each other through this process. When you commit yourself to action and others hold you accountable, you'll make progress much faster than you would on your own, when it's easier to make excuses. We all procrastinate on the things we're afraid of or dread or just aren't sure how to do well. Going through this

> process with a group will provide you with support, accountability, access to people in target organizations and a shorter learning curve.

Whitcomb, Susan Britton. ***Resume Magic, 4th Edition***. Indianapolis: JIST Publishing, 2010.

> By all means, to create the most effective resume that you can, get help in person and use a job outsourcing service if you have access to it. Also, see this book. There are as many opinions on resumes as there are books and advisors. That can be very frustrating. Remember that looking for a job *is* a job. Different jobs have different required tools and skills. A resume is a requirement, so educate yourself and get professional input from this book and/or from local professionals if you have such access.

I'd like to credit my colleague Judy Levy, MS, PCC, ORSCC for the following suggestions. When asked to contribute, Judy Levy replied, "I've been asked lately for my favorite go-to resources for job hunting. There are tons of them out there—and if you submit a query into your preferred search engine, you'll get a *lot* of answers. Many of the links are very helpful and you'll be able to target your search and get quick answers. But for general support, here's what I suggest:"

- Yale, Martin. ***Knock 'em Dead 2014: The Ultimate Job Search Guide***. Massachusetts: Adams Media, 2013.

  > Look for the ***Knock 'em Dead*** book series by Martin Yale. Yale provides great all-around reference for soup-to-nuts job search information that is updated annually with current websites. He is outstanding and provides lots of very practical help. See his website: www.Knockemdead.com.

- Cordcodilos, Nick. ***Ask the Headhunter: Reinventing the Interview to Win the Job***. New York: Plume, 1997.

  > Nick Cordcodilos has great advice and is featured on many shows and networks including PBS. Good stuff. See his website: www.asktheheadhunter.com.

- Lucas, Suzanne. *The Evil HR Lady* (blog). www.evilhrlady.org.

    Fun, irreverent, and very poignant HR information, including job search information.

- Ireland, Susan. *The Complete Idiot's Guide to the Perfect Resume*. California: Alpha Press, 2010.

    You'll find templates and examples for resumes in multiple disciplines. See her website: www.susanireland.com.

Job Posting Sites

I must admit: I have mixed feelings about putting a list of websites here. While you do need to know about *all* of your available resources—websites included—my concern is that you'll fall in to the trap of thinking, "All I need to do is sit at my computer and submit applications and resumes all day." You can't imagine how many job seekers have shown up at the networking groups and said they'd been doing just that, and *only* that, for six months and had heard nothing in return.

Please don't waste months *just* submitting applications to these sites. Combine that work with networking your way into an organization.

That said, these sites can be a useful supplement to your job search.

- www.careerbuilder.com
- www.careernet.com
- www.craigslist.net
- www.indeed.com
- www.job-hunt.com
- www.jobster.com
- www.linkup.com
- www.simplyhired.com
- www.theladders.com

There are many, many more sites. But this should be a good start. You can also search for sites specific to your industry.

Job Seeker Groups

I recommend that you visit several different job seeker groups and attend a couple that you really like weekly. Some of these events are speaker-based, some primarily hold workshops, and others are more focused on networking. Find the type of group that works best for you.

I've found that searching the Internet for phrases like these can yield good results and help you find groups in your area:

> job seeker groups *<your-town>*
> job seeker networking groups
> job seeker support groups

When You Don't Know What You Want to Do Next

Two highly experienced career counselors from the Bay Area, Judy Levy and Mary Lynne Schoenberg, recommend the following books and websites to their clients. They are two career coaches I would gladly recommend. You can probably find most of these in your library or purchase them used online.

- Bolles, Richard. ***What Color is Your Parachute 2015***. California: Ten Speed Press, 2014.

  A classic, solid book (and app) that's fabulous for helping people figure out what they want to do when they grow up. See his website: http://www.jobhuntersbible.com/

- Bolles, Richard and Carol Christen. ***What Color is Your Parachute? For Teens: Discovering Yourself, Defining Your Future***. California: Ten Speed Press, 2010.

- Bolles, Richard and John Nelson. ***What Color is Your Parachute? For Retirement: Planning a Prosperous, Healthy, and Happy Future***. California: Ten Speed Press, 2010.

Another experienced career counselor, Fay Krapf of Raleigh, NC, highly recommends the following books for this process of self-discovery and reinvention:

- Beck, Martha. ***Finding Your Way in a Wild New World: Reclaim Your True Nature to Create the Life You Want***. New York: Atria

Press, January 2013.

Martha provides you with a step-by-step program to guide you as you create your own ideal life. She will teach you how to read your internal compasses, articulate your core desires, and repair the unconscious beliefs that may be blocking your progress. Included are case studies, questionnaires, and exercises to guide you through the planning and implementation of a more satisfying life.

- Sher, Barbara. *I Could Do Anything If I Only Knew What It Was: How To Discover What You Really Want and How To Get It*. New York: Dell, 1995.

Barbara reveals how to, in her own words, "recapture long lost goals, overcome the blocks that inhibit your success, decide what you want to be, and live your dreams."

- Sher, Barbara. *Live the Life You Love: In Ten Easy Step-by-Step Lessons*. New York: Dell, 1997.

Barbara Sher's program is simple but can be truly transforming. She shows you how to break free from a work life that does not work for you, transform your thinking, and create a foundation for success that includes loving what you do and doing what you love.

Introverts and Extraverts

Laney, Marti Olsen. *The Introvert Advantage: How to Thrive in an Extrovert World*. New York: Workman Publishing, 2002.

Laney, Marti Olsen. *The Hidden Gifts of the Introverted Child*. New York: Workman Publishing, 2005.

I am very grateful to Marti Laney, Psy.D. When I came across her book, she brought my understanding of introverts to an entirely new level. Thanks to her work and my training in psychological type in general, I've been able to help job seekers understand how to handle interviews, networking, and taking care of themselves during a job transition.

I am a classic extravert myself, but I was raised by introverts—four of them: both parents, a grandmother, and my step-father. You would think that I would *understand* introverts since my childhood had been shaped by four of them. Unfortunately, they remained mysterious to me.

When I came to understand the power of psychological type, I saw the very logical reason for my lack of understanding. Even though I was surrounded by them, *I saw them through my own extraverted filter.* It wasn't until I became aware of this filter that I could empathize with or understand introverts. I regularly misinterpreted their intentions and did not make proper space for them in our conversations. Professionally, this field of research and application, along with the wonderful mentors I've had along the way, have empowered me to help many teams work more effectively together and to make managing people less mysterious and less painful for managers.

If you are interested in helping an introverted child navigate an extraverted world with more confidence and grace, I highly recommend her book on children.

Cain, Susan. Quiet, **The Power of Introverts in a World That Can't Stop Talking**. New York: Crown Publishers, 2012.

Susan Cain's work is invaluable. She's helpful to introverts trying to live in an extraverted world. She's equally helpful to extraverts who genuinely want to work better with introverts. Extraverts aren't intentionally being difficult; they just need help in knowing how to make space for introverts.

Introverts have a lot to contribute. It can be hard for them to be heard amidst the din of typical extraverts in action. If group behavior is not adjusted to make more space for introverts to contribute, then a lot of value is left out of the room when decisions are being made.

Please see my website, **www.effectivewithpeople.com**, for free downloads such as the following Tips Sheets for introverts and extraverts:

- Interview Tips for Introverts
- Interview Tips for Extraverts
- Networking Tips for Introverts
- Networking Tips for Extraverts
- Introverts During a Job Transition
- Extraverts During a Job Transition
- Communication Tips for Introverts and Extraverts.

Psychological Resources

Brown, Brené. ***Daring Greatly: How the Courage to Be Vulnerable Transforms the Way We Live, Love, Parent, and Lead***. New York: Gotham Books, 2012.

Brown, Brené. ***The Gifts of Imperfection***. Minnesota: Hazelden, 2010.

> Brené Brown, Ph.D., teaches that we are required to face and manage our shame triggers and learn how to be vulnerable in order to prosper in times that call for courageous acts. Today's economy and job market definitely call for courage.
>
> I hate to say that she's right—I didn't want her to be right. After all, no one likes to face their shame and be vulnerable. But Dr. Brown's findings after more than 10 years of research on shame are compelling. We ignore this research at our peril. The good news is that Dr. Brown has some powerful ideas about how to help us learn and heal our way through very difficult periods.
>
> I highly recommend both of these volumes, as well as her webinar on *The Gifts of Imperfection*.

Thompson, Henry (Dick) L. ***The Stress Effect, Why Smart Leaders Make Dumb Decisions—And What to Do About It***. New Jersey: Jossey-Bass, 2010.

> Henry (Dick) L. Thompson, Ph.D., is a trusted mentor and a not-

ed author and researcher in the field of psychological type. I'm listing this book because it taught me to respect the power of stress so that I can take care of myself in the face of it. Dealing with stress is not just about "being tough." It's about recognizing the powerfully negative bio-chemical effect that long-term stress can have on our brains so that we can take appropriate steps to care for ourselves. We cannot afford to ignore it or deny it or tell ourselves to "suck it up." The point is to get smarter about how we deal with it.

Achor, Shawn. *The Happiness Advantage: The Seven Principles of Positive Psychology that Fuel Success and Performance at Work*. New York: Crown Publishing Group, 2010.

I'm imagining what you're thinking, "I don't have a *job* and she wants me to read a book on *happiness?*" Yes, seriously, the field of positive psychology has powerful things to teach us about how we can help ourselves both feel better and perform more creatively and effectively.

This author spoke to a group in Zimbabwe when their economy was falling apart and they were struggling under a dictator. They listened with rapture. In 2008 after Lehman Brothers had collapsed, he also worked with AIG executives after they themselves had just become a ward of the Federal Reserve.

If executives in these circumstances found value in what Achor had to say, job seekers everywhere have a lot to learn about Achor's—and countless other researchers'—work with positive psychology. Being a job seeker in this market is incredibly challenging. We should use all the help we can get from whatever direction or field of research it may come.

Spiritual Resources

I do not have a particular agenda to push here. I'd simply like to list resources that have been uplifting and empowering to me during recent times of stress and challenge. The job seeking years were difficult, but I found strength and comfort in these books by both Christian and Buddhist authors. The first two books in particular were helpful during the years of starting my own business. I offer them in case they may prove helpful to you.

Osteen, Joel. ***I Declare: 31 Promises to Speak Over Your Life***. New York: Hachette Book Group, 2012.

Osteen, Joel. ***Your Best Life Begins Each Morning: Devotions to Start Each Day***. New York: Hachette Book Group, 2008.

> Joel Osteen was not even on my radar. I'm afraid I had a bit of a prejudice against "TV preachers." Luckily for me, a friend would forward me his positive daily message from time to time. She was also a job seeker, so she recognized when a particular message might apply and be especially uplifting. I was won over after the third email. Both of these volumes kept me uplifted and positive as I took on the daunting task of moving from a "Boomer job seeker" to a "Boomer new business owner." I read them every morning. I highly recommend both of these volumes if you are open to encouragement from a positive Christian perspective.

Chodran, Pema. ***When Things Fall Apart: Heart Advice for Difficult Times***. Boston: Shambala, 2002.

Chodran, Pema. ***Comfortable with Uncertainty: 108 Teachings on Cultivating Fearlessness and Compassion***. Boston: Shambala, 2005.

Chodran, Pema. ***The Places That Scare You: A Guide to Fearlessness in Difficult Times***. Boston: Shambala, 2005.

> Pema Chodran, an ordained Buddhist nun and notable teacher, does not seek to teach you how to make the fear and discomfort go away. She teaches you instead that those feelings are absolutely human and that you can best face them by consciously experiencing them instead of trying to avoid feeling them.
>
> This is not everyone's cup of tea, but I found it helpful when I first found myself without a job. I studied meditation for two years, every Monday night. I was in a state of shock at the time and

in the market for someone who would just make me feel better. For someone who was not offering to make the fear "go away," Chodran was surprisingly comforting and helpful. She brings compassion and understanding to fear and to the "hard times" experience.

Her recommendations are not unlike those of Brené Brown. When experiencing the sometimes overwhelming feelings that come with challenging times, there's no way *around the feelings*; the only way is *through them*. The sooner we stop the unconscious avoidance behaviors, the sooner we can move to productive behaviors and move forward in our lives.

About the Author

Carol A. Linden, speaker and author, is the principal consultant and owner of Effective With People, LLC. She is an MBTI Master Practitioner and, since 2004, has trained over 1,000 clients in Psychological Type, Temperament, and Interaction Styles. She is a Certified Professional Co-Active Coach (CPCC) and a member of the National Speaker's Association. She is also Adjunct Faculty at Wake Technical College.

In addition to this book, she has authored articles in *Bulletin of Psychological Type* and has spoken at four conferences of the Association of Psychological Type International (2009, 2011, 2013, and 2015). She speaks frequently to professionals in the field of psychological type.

This book comes out of her own experience of surviving a layoff and starting her own business, as well as four years of volunteering her time as a facilitator and workshop leader for a job seekers networking group that meets weekly in the RTP area of North Carolina.

There is life after the layoff.
In fact, there can be a better life.
I know that from personal experience.
After using this book, you will know it too.

For copies of her articles and helpful tip sheets, please see her website: www.effectivewithpeople.com. You may reach her for speaking engagements at info@effectivewithpeople.com.

CPSIA information can be obtained at www.ICGtesting.com
Printed in the USA
LVOW04s0549180615

442912LV00002B/2/P